NORFOLK RIVERS AND HARBOURS

Vol 5 English Estuaries Series

ROBERT SIMPER

Published in 1996 by Creekside Publishing
ISBN 0 9519927 5 9
copyright Robert Simper
Printed by The Lavenham Press Ltd
Lavenham, Suffolk

By the same author

Over Snape Bridge (1967)
Woodbridge & Beyond (1972)
East Coast Sail (1972)
Scottish Sail (1974)
North East Sail (1975)
Victorian & Edwardian Yachting from Old Photographs (1978)
Gaff Sail (1979)
Traditions of East Anglia (1980)
Suffolk Show (1981)
Britain's Maritime Heritage (1982)
Sail on the Orwell (1982)
Beach Boats of Britain (1984)
Sail: The Surviving Tradition (1984)
East Anglian Coast and Waterways (1985)
Suffolk Sandlings (1986)
The Deben River (1992)
The River Orwell and the River Stour (1993)
Rivers Alde, Ore and Blyth (1994)
Woodbridge: Pictorial History (1995)
Essex Rivers and Creeks (1995)

CONTENTS

Cover: The wherry *Albion* sailing towards
Thurne mouth.

ACKNOWLEDGEMENTS

The old local saying 'Norfolk do different' certainly applies to the maritime affairs of this county. That is because the conditions are unique. There is nowhere else quite like the Norfolk Broads. They are a complete self contained maritime world, while the ports and harbours around the coast all have their own very strong local character.

When I started to put together this record of the affairs on rivers and harbours I was almost overpowered by the number of books there are about the Norfolk Broads. Had I read all this vast library of books I would never have had time to write this book. However a book is a very good way of recording the history of an area because the information is then stored in more than one place. It was a very sad day for recorded history in Norfolk when on August 1 1994 the Central Library at Norwich was badly damaged by fire and books and records stored within it were destroyed.

I first went on the Broads in 1952 when my father bought the cabin cruiser *Merry Princess* at Wroxham. The next spring *Merry Princess* was moved down to the River Deben, but the impression I got of the Norfolk rivers was of continual bungalows along the waters edge while Wroxham Broad seemed a remote and rural place. When I came back in the 1970s I was amazed at the increase in the number of boats. Although some riverside pubs seemed to have gone down market and taken on a brash urban image. However the actual rivers and most of the places still retained the atmosphere of rural Norfolk.

In this attempt to sum up the history of the rivers, their boats and people I have drawn on the knowledge of many local people. On the early medieval history of Norwich I am indebted to Brian S.Ayers of the Norfolk Archaeological Unit for his paper 'The Growth of a Saxon Port'. Early drawings of Norwich show spritsail rigged craft. Mike Stammers,a Norfolk man now at the Merseyside Maritime Museum, points out that early nineteenth century paintings show small spritsail barges carrying tree to saw mills on the Yare above the New Mills. Theo Douglas Sherwoods efforts to save the last Norfolk keel brings us closer to another piece of the Broad's past.

The nostalgic images of the keels and wherries haunt the Broads and it is surprising that no one has built a smaller version of one of them. Vincent Pargeter with his heroic piece of quiet determination in rebuilding the *Maud* shows this

is within the realms of possibility.

Through its many ups and downs the Norfolk Wherry Trust has kept the wherry *Albion* sailing, no small achievement, and has also saved material about the wherry era. I am particularly gratefully to members of the Norfolk Wherry Trust for allowing me to draw on their collection of material about the 'old days' on the Broads when there was a steady stream of wherries sailing between the towns and parish staithes. James Forsythe, himself once a pleasure wherry owner, opened many doors here as well as passing on his own memories. The Forsythe family moved to Hickling in 1932 because the Thames had become too crowded. In his retirement James moved off to the Fens because Wroxham had become too crowded, but his time in Norfolk will always be remembered because of his guiding hand steering the Norfolk Wherry Trust. In the early years of the Trust it looked as if it would be impossible to keep an ageing wooden craft sailing, many members pulled out, Lady Beryl Mayhew, Humphrey Boardman and James Forsythe kept the Trust going.

The yacht designer John Perryman, who in recent decades has played a leading part in the Norfolk Wherry Trust, has kindly allowed me to draw from his great knowledge of wherries, yachts and forgotten staithes on silted up dykes. John started work at Herbert Woods between 1950-56 and learnt his trade from the legendary Jimmy Turner and his basic naval architecture from Cliff Patchet and the yard designer John Loynes.

Mike Sparkes, one of the seven people who take turns to skipper the *Albion*, has passed on a great deal of knowledge about the upper Yare and wherries generally. It was only after he got evolved with the Trust that he discovered his ancestors had been Norwich wherrymen and a great grandfather, Stephen Field, a Thorpe boat builder. The wherry age has now slipped over the horizon, but fortunately Roy Clark gathered together many first hand accounts of the 'old days' which appeared in his much admired book *Black Sail Traders*.

An expert in recognising wherries is Nigel Royall. His family were wherrymen at Norwich and they had a boatyard on Kings Street before moving up to Hoveton in the 1960s. Here they operate a fleet of eighteen hire craft, but in the winter Nigel maintains the pleasure wherry *Solace* when she returns to their 'boat shod'. Just across the Bure Peter Bower of Wroxham was also most willing to supply information on wherry yachts. Jane and Peter Tracy made family material on Barton Broad available. Other material came from Dave Barrett on Halvergate Marshes and Olga Sinclair on Potter Heigham.

On the port of Norwich Bryan Read was most helpful. His family milling business was heavily involved with shipping on the Yare. He took photographs of the everyday events when shipping came up to Norwich, but how soon they became history. At Reedham Tony and Steve Sanderson were very helpful with the story of their yard. On the Broads yachts I have to thank Alan Dunn who started the Vintage Wooden Boat Association in 1987 and has restored two Broads yachts *Corsair* and then the *Pollywog*.

Mark Wells, owner of the Norfolk Rivers yacht *Melody*, came up with many helpful suggestions on how to unravel the story of the rivers and broads. The commercial craft were quite separate to the yachts and the hire boats and private yachts followed different lines of development. However all these craft, coasters, wherries, yachts and hire craft all sail the same waters even though they have very different stories.

The Maritime Museum at Yarmouth started to get together a collection of Norfolk craft and my thanks to Damion Eaton for showing them to us. All these are presevered but hopefully one day they will actually be seen by the public. I thank the Broads Authority and the Eastern Sea Fishery for their help.

The Haven Bridge at Yarmouth is the border between two very different worlds. The inland waterways of the Broads river system are a gentle world of reed lined banks, waterside pubs and farmland, while below the bridge there are harsh unforgiving tidal conditions. The coastal harbours of north Norfolk are lovely places in the good weather in the summer, but in an onshore gale they are death traps. Yet both these worlds are part of Norfolk.

When ever possible I prefer to use photographs to try and recall the past because providing they have not been touched up they are totally accurate. However sometimes it is possible to recreate the past with drawings. For the illustrations I have to thank Ken Lockwood, Harry Clow of Thurston, Mike Sparkes and also my daughter Caroline Southernwood. All of them for their patience in drawing and redrawing to get them ascorrect as we could. Thanks once again to Geoff Cordy for the photographic work. My wife Pearl has shared the many delightful facets of exploring the Broads and coastline and helped with the unseen work in pulling together the final project.

This is the fifth book in the English Estuaries Series and I have to say the people of Norfolk were particularly helpful. Perhaps this is because they are used to helping the summer visitors. Anyway, this is very much their story.

RS
Ramsholt

Source of Illustrations
Bryan Read 1, 2, 13, 14, 15, 16, 17, 18, 128. Norfolk Wherry Trust 3, 21, 32, 33, 36, 60, 66, 76, 78, 88, 89, 118, 121. Michael Sparkes 61, 59, 90, 91. Harry Clow 7, 8. Graham Newman 12, 125, 126, 127. James Forsythe 19, 24, 50, 51, 52, 53, 54, 55, 65, 77, 82, 92, 93, 107, 108, 110, 112. Lady Beryl Mayhew 22, 23, 63, 64, 116. Steve Sanderson 34, 37, 38, 39, 40, 41, 69, 104. Demaus 62, 70, 71, 72, 73. K. C. Lockwood 58, 79. Tim Childs 81. Peter and Jayne Tracey 83, 84, 85, 149. Alan Dunn 97, 98, 99, 100. John Perryman 48. Ivan Gould 49. Eastern Daily Press 102. East Anglian Daily Times 109. Yarmouth Maritime Museum 122, 131. Douglas Went 135. Michael Ward 148. Photographs from 1955 onwards were taken by the author and others are from his collection.

Chapter One
THE NORWICH RIVER

1. The New Mills, Norwich with a wherry alongside St Swithin's Flour Mill in 1880. Although it was tidal up to the New Mills so much fresh water came down that the wherries were always going against the current to reach these mills. In order to get wherries up here there were a series of posts at the sides of the river from Trowse Eye to the New Mills so that they could be hauled around difficult bends.

2. St Swithin's Mill, with the wherry *Volunteer* of Langley alongside, in about 1900. In 1896 R.J.Read's mill at Beccles was burnt down so he purchased St Swithin's mill at Norwich. St Swithin's closed in 1936 when Reads moved to King Street.

Reads owned the wherry *Goodwill* which took flour to their depots at Beccles and Horstead and brought imported wheat up from Gt Yarmouth. They sold the *Goodwill* in 1926 for £90 to the General Steam Navigation Co who took on a contract to continue Reads work for three years. At this time the company were buying up the wherries in order to reduce competition for their fleet of tugs and lighters which they operated between Yarmouth and Norwich.

3. William Hobrough's wherries being used to help build the Whitefriars Bridge, Norwich in 1925.

4. The Cow Tower, at Norwich with wherries in about 1912. These wherries are the larger Norwich River high stern-sheet wherries which did not have a cockpit aft. The Cow Tower on the Hospital Meadow was built in 1278 and rebuilt about 1370 as part of the extensive fortification of the city.

In the medieval period sea going ships were navigated even further up to Fye Bridge. The Anglo Saxon Kings of East Anglia had their 'Northern Market' in Tombland, while the southern market was at Ipswich. To get to the Northern market Anglo-Saxon ships were discharged near St Martin-at-Palace Plain. Here they ran up on a shingle spit and goods were carried ashore on bush wood walkways. Medieval sea going ships stopped coming up to Norwich in about 1300.

5. Pull's Ferry in about 1910 with a Norfolk boat being used as a ferry. The ferry took its name from the sixteenth century ferryman John Pull. In the background is the fifteenth century water gate which guarded the canal that ran up to the Lower Close and had been used to bring up stone for building the cathedral. The last ferryman Ceil Mollett gave up in 1943. The watergate which was part of the city wall was restored in 1947.

6. Bread being delivered in a Norwich street during the Floods of 1912. Over three inches of heavy rain fell in a few hours which caused the east Norfolk rivers to burst their banks. The streets of Norwich had been flooded before in November 1878 when three inches of snow thawed quickly followed by heavy rain.

9. The transom stern of the 54ft Norfolk keel which was raised from the Whitlingham Marshes by Theo Douglas-Sherwood's team in 1985. After this the Norfolk Keel Trust started an up hill battle to save the craft. This keel appears to have been the one used with the dredger by J.S.Hobrough before being sunk about 1890 at Whitlingham Marshes to support the bank .

From the deck lay out of this keel it would appear they could haul the luff of the square sail down hard in order to sail close to the wind. This particlar craft had very low sides and probably only loaded about 30 tons, while the wherry *Albion* loaded around 40 tons.

Opposite Above. 7. This is Harry Clow's drawing of Norfolk keels on the Norwich River. So little is known about the keels that it is difficult to to be precise about their details.

The keel was the inland cargo craft of the Broads before the wherry. The Norfolk keel's clinker (over lapping planks) construction suggests that these craft evolved from the Anglo-Saxon sea going craft and like all early medieval craft they had a single square sail. When the Broads were dug to provide peat for household fires it was the keels that were used to transport it up to Norwich. The early keels would also have shipped the stone up for building churchs. Since there were keels in used from about 800 to 1890 they were a common sight in Norfolk for over a thousand years.

Even less is known of another type of Norfolk working craft, the barges which carried passengers between Yarmouth and Norwich until the late eighteenth century. They had hulls like the keels, but like many early Norfolk Rivers craft set a spritsail.

8. Harry Clow's drawing of a Norfolk keel being loaded with reeds. In the early nineteenth century there were around fifty keels trading between Yarmouth and Norwich, but they were replaced by the handier wherries. The last keel could have been the *Dee Dar* which until about 1889 was bringing timber to Hospital Meadow in the centre of Norwich.

10. Wherries at Norwich in 1913. This was looking down river from Bishop's Bridge with the tannery, noted for it's strong smell, on the left. The lighter *Expectation* is being towed down. She may have been one of the lighters used to bring coal from Yarmouth to Norwich Gas Works. The last of these lighters was towed away in 1961.

Norwich was the centre of the wherry trade and John Perryman has worked out that throughout the nineteenth century around two hundred wherries were owned in Norwich and a further hundred around the Broads. To keep the wherry fleet sailing a considerable back up of boat builders and merchants were needed so that at the height of the wherry trade in the mid Victorian period around 2400 men would have relied on them for an income.

The early wherries came from the Thames and were lightly built open transom sterned rowing boats hired out to carry one or two passengers. Because the rowing wherries were fast, larger versions were built to carry cargoes. The first cargo wherries had spritsails, by the Elizabethan era gaff sails began to be used, but were still set on a mast stepped right forward in the bow. At some point, probably in the late eighteenth century, an enterprizing owner put a weight on the foot of a wherry's mast to make it counter balance so that the mast could be lowered easily. This made the gaff wherry the most effective craft trading on the Norfolk rivers and the keel and barge dropped out of favour. In the wherry age from around 1750 to 1920 they were a competitive form of transport in eastern Norfolk

11. Looking down the River Wensum from Foundry Bridge in about 1925. The barge on the right is Everard's sailing barge *Scotia*. Sailing barges were usually towed up from Yarmouth although if one of their coasters was in the river they towed them up. The only barge remembered as sailing against the wind to Norwich was Everard's *Sara* and it took her two days.

6

12. Looking up river from the new Carrow Road Bridge in 1932. On the left the steamer *River Witham* is being discharged of coal by hand at Raymond Coller's coal yard. Further up stream another collier is discharging coal at Moy's wharf, while on the right is the tanker *Angloco* which used to bring fuel up from Lowestoft.

Between the two colliers the 1000 ton grain silo at R.J.Read's Albion flour mill is taking shape. In order to take advantage of the small motor coasters which came up to Norwich, Jack and Hector Read purchased a yarn mill on King Street, which had been built in 1836, and moved their flour mill from Westwick Street which was above the fixed bridges. As well as bringing in imported wheat, the silo also enabled the firm to import maize for use in animal feed.

In the Victorian period country mills were grinding locally grown wheat, but when cheap imported wheat became available millers switched to this and mills were sited at the ports. This imported wheat was also more suitable for flour, but after the World War II grain shortages had ended, East Anglian farmers began to grow varieties of milling wheat suitable for breadmaking. When Britain entered the European Common Market this encouraged millers to use home grown wheat and by the end of the 1980s many port side mills had closed.

13. The steamer *Moorlands* arriving at the main berth at R.J.Read's flour mill in 1958. She was the last steamer to bring a cargo to Norwich.

In 1833 the Norwich and Lowestoft Navigation reopened the port of Norwich to sea going vessels but a very limited number of ships came up until the Carrow Road lifting bridge was opened in 1923 and Corporation Quay was established on Riverside Road. This allowed ships to go to wharves as far as Foundry Bridge, but traffic on the river increased even more after the Norwich Power Station was opened in 1926.

14. Looking up river from Carrow Road Bridge in 1961 with Sully's wooden sailing barge *Beatrice Maud* on the left discharging at Read's and the Danish motor ship *Gruno* at Read's main berth.

Carrow Road lifting Bridge replaced the foot ferry which had been there while the old Carrow Road Bridge, built in 1810 had been lower down river.

15. Looking past Trowse Eye where the rivers Yare and Wensum meet, in 1968. On the left a German coaster is going up river while Metcalf's *Monica M* and Everard's *Spontaneity* are on the Power Station berths.

The average sized ship which came up to Norwich loaded about 350 tons, but ships of up to 500 tons could come up. The ships going to the Power Station drew 11ft of water, but because of a pipe across the river bed only ships of around 10ft draft could go above Carrow Road Bridge. Further up river on the bend above Read's there was a Turning Berth for ships of 150 ft in waterline length or 165ft if they had flared bows. Ships larger than this were towed down to Trowse Eye for turning.

16. The Norwich bucket dredger *Russell* in 1960 shortly before she was scrapped. Only a little dredging went on at the bends as normally the ships that came up to Norwich washed the channel clear. Will Everard used to say that when his ships went into dry dock he could always tell the ones that had been trading regularly to Norwich because their bottoms were shinny.

17. During the hard winter of 1962-3 five ships were held up at Reedham waiting to go down stream while two were waiting to get up to Norwich. Here Everard's 175ft *Sincerity* bound up river tried to get past the Railway Bridge, but was unable to force her way through the ice.

18. Everard's 500 gross ton 163ft *Spontaneity* approachs Reedham bound down river light from the Norwich Power Station. After 1923 the tonnage landed at Norwich steadily increased until it reached a peak of 250000 tons in 1964. The real decline in the river trade came with the closure of the coal burning Power Station in 1976. The Dock Labour Scheme kept Norwich viable because Yarmouth, which was in the scheme, had to employ more dockers than it needed thus making it very expensive. Some Yarmouth firms at times found it cheaper to send cargo up to Norwich and then have it brought back by road. When the Dock Labour Scheme was abolished and ships grew larger, the port of Norwich declined very quickly. The last coastal ship up here appears to have been the 345grt *Boekanier* in about 1988.

19. The wherry *Albion* being loaded with trees opposite Thorpe Green in 1950. Two copses on the Crown Point Estate had been cut down and the trees were being taken to Beccles. The mast is canted aft so that the trees could be swung aboard. Roy Clark, author of *Black Sail Traders*, and mate George 'Shackles' Cates are working the winch while skipper Jack Cates is guiding the tree trunk. Jack Cates was also the last Norwich River pilot.

The 58ft *Albion* was built in 1898 and was the only carvel built wherry. During World War II *Albion* was used for storage at Colman's Carrow Works and luckily just survived the bombing on Norwich in 1942 in which the wherry *Eudora* was destroyed. When the Norfolk Wherry Trust was set up in 1949 they bought *Albion*, rigged her out again and started trading her, but it proved impossible to get her to pay her way by carrying freights. The Norfolk Wherry Trust, supported by many businesses and organizations, have overcome many problems with *Albion* and kept her sailing. This Trust has become the inspiration for many others which have been set up to save traditional craft.

20. The pleasure steamer *Water Fly* taking passengers on a trip down the Yare past Thorpe in about 1910. The *Water Fly* was launched in 1896 and in the summer week days carried passengers from Yarmouth to Norwich and at the weekend made trips from Yarmouth to St Olaves. She was abandoned on Breydon Water in 1914.

The first Thorpe Water Frolic was held in 1821. John Harvey started the Frolic to give the Norwich cloth workers a day out. The rowing and other events were watched by crowds of up to 20000, the gentry on the north bank and the working people on the south bank.

21. The wherry *Meteor* being loaded with bricks at the brickworks next to Surlingham Ferry about 1908.

22. The spoon bowed 29ft *Castanet* built by George Mollett at Brundall in 1892 revolutionized Broadland racing. Previously Broads yachts had been shallow draft copies of their sea going sisters, indeed many from the Norwich River were built to sail on the Broads and the open sea. The *Castanet's* 'skimming dish' hull completely broke away from the old straight stemmed yacht and was a purely inland waterways craft. The following year Mollett tried another revolutionary yacht with the 29ft centreboarder *Zingara*. She was not nearly so successful, but she survived and was still sailing in 1995.

23. Russell Colman owner of the *Castanet* at the foot of the mast with his boatman Parker on the bow. The *Castanet's* builder George Mollett had moved his yard down to Brundall from Pull's Ferry, Norwich.

24. Major James Forsythe's pleasure wherry *Bramble* leaving Coldham Hall in 1951. She was a North River wherry which was originally called the *Empress of India*. This pleasure wherry ended up at the Martham boatyard and was eventually broken up in 1958.

25. John Royal on his 27ft wherry rigged *Maid of the Mist* at the 1994 Vintage Wooden Boat Association rally at Brundall. The *Maid of the Mist* was built as the Sheringham crabber *Marion* in 1926 and John bought her as a hulk. In 1990 he converted her to the wherry rig and renamed her after the little wherry that P.H.Emerson had cruised in when he photographed the Broads.

26. The 42ft Broads motor cruiser *Princess of Light* at the 1994 Vintage Wooden Boat rally at Brundall. This cruiser was built by Herbert Woods at Potter Heigham in 1937. Broads cruisers appear to have started off with cockpits in their bows but by the 1920s stern cockpits had been adopted. The design developed on to have centre cockpits in the 1930s.

Herbert Woods was a very innovative designer of Broads yachts, motor cruisers and sailing punts. He designed his motor cruisers so that they left little wash to prevent damage to the banks. They all had the word *light* in their names. *Twilight* and *Delight* were small cruisers while *Queen of Light*, one of the larger ones, was built for his wife.

27. Norfolk Rivers class yachts at Coldham Hall just before the start of the 1986 Yare Navigation Race. This annual race was started in 1976.

The rebirth of racing on the Broads encouraged the pattern of boat ownership to change. In 1977 there were 11632 boats licensed on the Broads, of which 3897 were hire craft. After this there was a steady decline in the number of hire craft which was down to 2445 by 1995. However the private craft had increased from 7735 in 1977 to 10640 in 1995, making a total of 13085 licensed boats.

28. The *Forester*, *Ladybird* and *White Wings* at the start of the 1979 Yare Navigation Race. In this race the skippers chose when they started to try and get the best possible wind and tide conditions. The winner was the fastest over the course on handicap time.

29. Tim Child's 32ft Broads yacht *White Wings* with A.D. Knights' *Ladybird* in the 1979 Yare Navigation Race .

The *White Wings* was built in 1928 after yacht designs had progressed through the late Victorian experiments such as *Castanet* and evolved into the classic Broads yacht. Most Broads yachts have kept to the gaff rig because it allows them to set a topsail to catch the wind coming over the tree tops. Unique features of the Broads yachts are the well aft, for the mainsheet man to stand in, the cabin sides that can be raised,the practice of setting the topsail before the mainsail is hoisted, and the eyelets in the mainsail for reef lacing.

THE YARE — CANTLEY.

30. Yachts racing off the 'Red House' at Cantley about 1911. Because the middle reaches of the Yare were free from trees this provided the best place for yacht racing. The Yare Sailing Club was formed at a meeting held in a Norwich boat shed in 1876 and quickly grew so that in twenty years it had 600 members and claimed to be the world's largest sailing club. The yachts took part in the races from Cantley to Breydon Water and even out to sea. In 1937 the YSC was one of several Broads clubs which linked up to form the Norfolk Broads SC at Wroxham. This took most of the racing up to the North River, but after the success of the Yare Navigation Race the Yare SC was reformed in 1987.

Red House, Cantley.

31. A 'timber lugging' wherry going up past Cantley in about 1905 and nodoubt bound up to Norwich. The wherry-men used to say that a wherry sailed best with 'just enough water on deck for a sparrow to get a drink'.

Ernest Woods' boat shed used to stand where the sugar beet factory silos are. Ernest Woods, brother of Potter Heigham's Walter Woods, was born in 1887 and trained as a shipwright at Cobholm, Great Yarmouth. He then set up a boatyard at Cantley. In 1908 he designed a 20ft Yare and Bure Sailing Club one-design and went on to built these day racers which are better known as the White Boats. However in 1927 because the centre of yachting had moved up to the North River, Ernest Woods moved to Horning. Everything in the yard was loaded into two wherries and it took two days to get round there. He continued building wooden yachts, cruisers and punts until he died in 1963 just after completing his sixty-ninth White Boat. The first fibre glass White Boat was made in 1981 and this gave the class a new lease of life bringing the number up to about 120 boats in 1995.

32. A wherry at Cantley Sugar Factory about 1920. The wherries brought in sugar beet from the farms and if their holds were clean wherries sometimes took sugar in bags down to Yarmouth. Motor wherries and barges brought in sugar beet to the factory until the 1964-65 campaign.

In the early years of the factory, which was very important to the local rural economy, sugar beet were brought by sailing barges from Suffolk rivers such the Deben. In 1955 Everard's sailing barge *Will Everard* was bringing freights of sugar beet from the Isle of Wight. Once when she made a slow passage due to bad weather the beet were rotten when the hatches were opened. While Everard's coasters used to load sugar at Cantley after discharging coal at Norwich.

33. The iron wherry *Uranus* at Loddon. In 1884 Arthur Sadd had the River Chet to Loddon dug deeper and wider by hand so that wherries could get up to his seed mills and wool warehouses at the head of the navigation. Woods, Sadd & Moore later had their own small wherries working up to these warehouses just below the mill. Woods, Sadd, Moore & Co closed about 1966 after which their warehouses on either side of the Chet head were pulled down for the Loddon boatyard and a new staithe constructed for visiting hire cruisers. The Loddon water mill remained but was badly damaged by fire in 1974.

REEDHAM FERRY.

No. 1135.

34. A wherry and yacht passing Reedham Ferry about 1903. The horse ferry on the Reedham bank was wound across the river by hand on 236ft of chain. At this time a small rowing boat was used for putting foot passengers across.

35. Reedham Ferry in 1972. It is probable that there was a ford here in the medieval period, but when the marshes on either banks were reclaimed the river became deeper. From the 1600s a ferry was crossing the Yare.

Norman Archer of the 'Ferry Inn' took over running the ferry in 1949 and later had an engine installed to haul the ferry across. To cater for sugar beet lorries a new ferry, 7ft longer was built by Newson's at Oulton Broad in 1986. When large ships, such as the tanker *Blackheath* went up to Cantley, the chains had to be lowered to the river bed. By 1995 Jim Stone, one of the ferryman, had worked here for nearly thirty years, while owner David Archer claimed it was the smallest car ferry in England.

36. Halls yard at Reedham about 1900 with two wherries hauled out for repair.

37. The Broads hire cruiser *Lady Wanderer*, built on the lines of a launch, was completed by Sandersons at Reedham in 1932. When steam launches first appeared on the Broads the builders gave them the lines of sailing craft but when they came to build the first motor cruisers the builders made launches with cabins fitted.

38. Sandersons yard at Reedham about 1938. This was the yard where the Hall family built wherries until about 1910. These included the wherry *Maud* and pleasure wherries *Solace* and *Hathor*. After World War I Charles Harris started yacht building and boat hiring from here and this business was bought by H.J.W.Sanderson of Cambridge in 1932.

Here about 1938 are the first three hire cruisers built and owned by Herbert James Walter Sanderson and his son Rupert 'Tony'. Left to right are the hire cruisers *Lady Brenda*, *Lady Pamela* and *Lady Monica*. Before 1939 they also built the cruisers *Ladybird*, *Albatross* and *Lady Ursula*. At the beginning of World War II most of Broads hire boats were moored on the Broads to prevent German sea planes landing an invasion force. Left out on the Broads most of these craft sank or rotted away. H.J.W.Sanderson talked his way out of sending his craft to the Broads by promising that he would burn his craft if the Germans landed. In this way the Sanderson craft survived the war and were brought out again for hire.

In the late 1940s there was a tremendous demand for new and hire boats but for several years it was impossible to get the wood. In 1960 Sanderson resumed building wooden cruisers , the 30ft Sandpiper class and the 20ft Sandlings class of hire cruisers, for their fleet until 1971. After this they fitted out the motor sailer *Sand Star* in 1971 and the 32ft *Sand Storm* in 1992. In 1995 Tony's two sons divided the business, Colin took the hire fleet and Steve the Old Hall Yard for specialist yacht repair.

39. The 22 ft motor cruiser *Albatross* being unloaded on Yarmouth quay ready for transhipment to Hong Kong. This was one of the Sanderson's *Lady* class cruisers with a Morris Vedette petrol engine which they were building at Reedham when an order came for a boat from a Chinese merchant.

40. On the left is H.J.W.Sanderson with son Rupert 'Tony', second right, with the family of one of their hirers. The cruiser is the *Lady Kathleen* built at Reedham in 1931. She had a petrol Ailsa Craig engine which gave the yard quite a lot of problems.

41. Reedham about 1900 with the old railway bridge swung on the village side. On the left is a wherry hauled up in a dock, long since filled in, near the 'Ship Inn'. Bound up the river is a Victorian Broads straight stemmed cutter yacht. Technically these yachts, with their single jibs, were sloops, but they were always referred to as being the cutters.

42. Danish coaster bound up river after passing Reedham railway bridge in 1986

43. The 32ft Broads yacht *Ladybird* being towed past the Reedham Railway Bridge during the 1979 Yare Navigation Race. In this race yachts clocked out of the race while they passed through the bridge and clocked in on the other side.

44. Below Reedham railway bridge about 1910 with the timber mill on the far bank in the distance. The lighter on the right appears to have one of Hobrough's dydling machines on it. Dydling means clearing out the side of a river. On smaller dykes this was done with hand tools.

45. The Broads yachts *Melody* and *Goldfish* passing the Berney Arms windmill in the Yare Navigation Race in 1986. This race was over a 30 mile course from Coldham Hall SC down to Breydon Water and back. The Victorian Broads yachts used to go down the coast to race at the Regattas, but the last Broads yacht to race at sea was the *Forester* in 1956.

46. Henry Hewitt of the 'Berney Arms' with the wherry *Albion* sailing past in the background in 1949.

47. The *Cuckoo* entering Breydon Water in the 1986 Yare Navigation Race which she went on to win. The *Cuckoo* started this Yare race in a westerly breeze which carried her all the way down to Breydon where she rounded the turning buoy at dead low water. At the same time the land heating up brought in an easterly breeze so that she was able to run back up to Coldham Hall. She was the first boat to make the fastest time, and win the Yare Race on handicap.

The Broads yachts are lightly built and carry a great press of sail. They have shallow draft and long keels which make them highly manoeuvrable. The 36ft *Cuckoo*, built of grp in 1982, has a keel about 12 ft long .

47a. Motor Cruisers at Loddon in 1974.

Chapter Two

HADDISCOE CUT AND THE RIVER WAVENEY

48. The pleasure wherry *Zoe* in the Haddiscoe New Cut about 1910. The New Cut was completed in 1833 and was part of a grand plan to make Norwich a port for sea going vessels. Before this all goods had been transhipped at Yarmouth and taken up river by keel or wherry. This meant that the merchants of Yarmouth controlled the trade to Norwich which was bitterly resented in the city. When a Norwich syndicate proposed to build a harbour at Lowestoft and a navigation linking it to Norwich it was Yarmouth's turn to protest vigorously. However the harbour, Mutford Lock and the New Cut were constructed and the first ship, the collier brig *Luna*, arrived at Norwich in 1833. Norwich did become a port but most of the ships came up via Yarmouth.

49. The wherry *Albion* after passing under Haddiscoe Bridge in the New Cut in 1983 as part of the 150 years anniversary of the Norwich and Lowestoft Navigation.

50. The pleasure wherry *Hathor* at Burgh Castle for the 1951 Wherry Race on Breydon Water. After the Norfolk Wherry Trust started trading the *Albion* there was great enthusiam to restart the wherry races, but these did not last for long because all the wherries and pleasure wherries were showing their age and the Broads were becoming very crowded with boats.

51. Albert 'Chuchy' Grimes, skipper of the pleasure wherry *Hathor* in the 1951 wherry race on Breydon Water.

52. The crew of the wherry *Albion* before the 1951 wherry race. This group includes skipper Jack Cates on the left and Nat Bircham who had the motor trading wherry *I'll Try* and was later skipper of the *Albion*.

53. The crew of the pleasure wherry *Hathor* before the 1951 wherry race. Front row include left to right Christopher Boardman, T. Pitcher, skipper A. Grimes. Back row includes left to right Jayne Forsythe, Diana Forsythe, James Forsythe, Humphrey Boardman in the yachting cap and Walter Cates at the far end.

54. The pleasure wherry *Dragon* sailing to the start of the 1951 wherry race with *Albion* and *Hathor* in the background. The *Dragon* was built in 1901 at Wroxham by the Norfolk Broads Yachting Co. This public company was set up to cater for the growing demand for Broads holidays encouraged by books and articles by writers such as G. Christopher Davies. The company bought three yards on the Broads and started to build up a hire fleet. This company finished in 1920 by which time the yards had been sold to their managers.

55. In 1952 a wherry race was held on Breydon Water in strong winds and the *Albion's* mast broke. In this photograph, taken during the same race the pleasure wherry *Hathor* has run aground on Breydon Water and the 22ft quants were not having much effect. Major James Forsythe is seen pushing her off, while Sir Basil Mayhew is watching from near the mast. The pleasure wherry *Dragon* also ran aground. After these mishaps the *Hathor* eventually won.

56. The 59ft wherry yacht *White Moth* sailing on the Waveney near Burgh St Peter in 1994. The *White Moth* was built in 1915 by Ernest Collins at Wroxham and was the last wherry yacht built. She was in the Collins hire fleet and sailed until 1956 when she became a houseboat. In 1985 Colin Facey bought the sunken wreck at St Olaves, took her back to his Horning yard and totally rebuilt her. In 1990 *White Moth*, after 20,000 boatyard hours of work, re-entered the hire fleet. After this she joined Mike Barnes' Norfolk Broads Yacht Co.

57. Geldeston Lock about 1904. Although Geldeston is the limit of navigation, it was one of three locks built which allowed wherries to get up to Bungay. The bar across the top was to prevent wherries from sailing in and damaging the lock. The last wherry to take a freight up to Bungay was the *Albion* and the lock was in use until 1934.

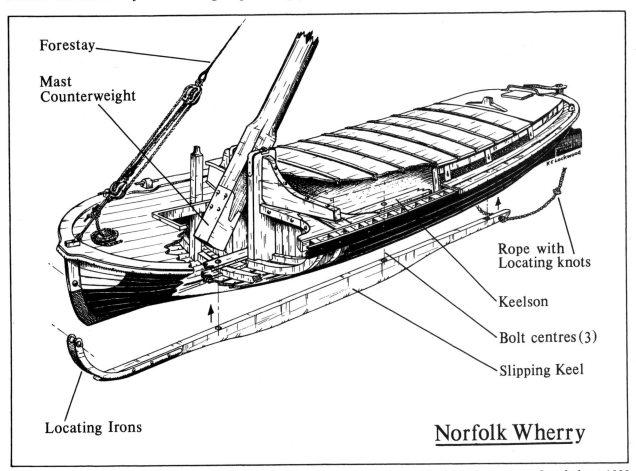

Forestay

Mast
Counterweight

Rope with
Locating knots

Keelson

Bolt centres (3)

Slipping Keel

Locating Irons

Norfolk Wherry

58. A Norfolk wherry showing how the slipping keel was fitted. The slipping keel which was introduced about 1880 gave the shallow draft wherry a grip on the water which improved the ability to sail against the wind. However to get up the shallow navigations the keel had to be unshipped at places such as Geldeston Lock and then reshipped when they came back down again. Wherry skipper Nat Bircham recalled it once took him four hours to reship a keel.

RIVERS YARE, WAVENEY,CHET,WENSUM AND THE NEW CUT

1. Burgh Castle was part of a chain of forts built by the Romans to defend East Anglia against Saxon pirates. Portland Cement Works beside the river here from 1859-1880. This cement works used mud dredged from the river.

2. In the 1860s the Reedham Cement Works was between the 'Berney Arms' and the windmill. The Berney family owned most of the land in this area in the late nineteenth century.

3. Berney Arms windmill is the largest windmill on the Norfolk Rivers. It was built in 1865 to replace an earlier mill. On the second floor it had vertical stones to grind cement clinkers from the adjoining cement works.

4. Halvergate Marshes. This vast marsh was traditionally used for summer grazing for livestock. As this form of farming became uneconomic in the 1980s landowners and farmers wanted to go over to arable agriculture which meant draining the whole area. Conservationists bitterly opposed this and fought a long campaign to stop the drainage. In 1988 a very sensible compromise was reached in which Halvergate became the first Environmentally Sensitive Area. The Government encouraged farmers to continue grazing the marshes in the traditional grazing way and helped out with the shortfall in return.

5. The Fleet across Halvergate Marshes had a river wall on either side. Before the pumping station was built the water level was managed by wind pumps. In the winter, water was lifted up and stored between The Fleet walls until the sluice opened at low tide and let the water out into Breydon. In the summer, water was stored between the walls and then pumped back on the marshes for the cattle to drink. In 1995 Dave Barrett, the RSPB warden of the 2000 acres on Halvergate, built a wind pump mill to pump water back from the Fleet to raise water levels during the summer.

6. Hardley Cross was erected in 1543 where the River Chet meets the Yare. The Yare above this point was under the control of Norwich while below, it was controlled by Yarmouth. The Yare was such an important trade link between Norwich and Yarmouth that the aldermen inspected the river every year. They met at Hardley Cross.

7. Hardley grazing marshes were abandoned after the 1953 Flood. There was an idea that this would prevent further flooding. However this was not the case as marshes were flooded twice in the next two decades below Carlton.

8. Hardley Dyke. The medieval dyke was a winding channel to the east of the present straight dyke. The present Hardley Dyke was dug about 1830. In 1850 James Bellward ran a coal business in warehouses at the head of the dyke while Mrs Bellward kept the 'Staithe House' public house. In 1995 the dyke was privately owned and the berths let out to private yacht owners.

9. Cantley Sugar Beet Factory started in 1912. Upstream of the Red House there was a dyke to a wherry staithe. Cantley Ferry used to run from below the sugar beet factory to the Round House.

10. Langley Dyke was dug to serve the medieval abbey. In Victorian times there was a flint warehouse and wherry staithe at the head of the dyke.

11. Hassingham Staithe below the church appears to have been used by wherries until about 1845 when the railway construction closed the dyke. In 1838 Buckenham and Hassingham Broads were connected, but since walling off from the tidal water they have become largely overgrown with reeds.

12. Old Buckenham Fen was cut for reeds by farmer John Askew until the drought summer of 1976 when the scrub became established. In 1995 volunteer conservationist cleared the Fen to re-establish reedbeds for birds habit.

13. Buckenham Ferry. A horse ferry, a large floating platform hauled across on chains by a windlass, operated until about 1936. Cars went across for one shilling (5p). During World War II the army had a floating pontoon bridge across here for troop movement in case there was an invasion. This was removed at night.

14. Strumpshaw Broad has silted up and is an RSPB reserve, but in the late eighteenth century keels and wherries were using a staithe on the broad .

15. Coldham Hall. Local legend has it that Queen Anne gave this place its name when she came down the river on a pleasure trip on a cold winters day. Coldham Hall was built in the eighteenth century as a shooting lodge and was later converted to the public house.

16. Coldham Hall Sailing Club started in 1951, but regattas had been held here in the late eighteenth century. From about 1830 rowing races were popular. Billy Breach ran a rowing foot ferry here until about 1955.

17. Surlingham Broad. All the medieval peat digging filled with rain water and had to be abandond. The 1839 Surlingham Tithe map still showed the ownership of the broad divided up into the narrow medieval peat digging strips. There was a wherry staithe at the west end near the road to the 'Ferry' pub, but the broad has largely overgrown.

18. Wheatfen Broad. This is the northern end of Rockland Broad which has largely silted up with reeds. The entrance to Wheatfen was blocked when the naturalist Ted Ellis brought the carvel pleasure wherry *Liberty* here and she sank.

19. Rockland Broad. In 1908 Sir Charles Rich, Lord of the Manor, tried to prevent angling on Rockland, but a court ruled that as it was tidal the public had the right to fish there. In 1952 the rhond or river wall broke and flooded the marshes to Claxton.

20. Rockland St Mary Staithe. In the nineteenth century this was used by wherries, often owned by the landlord of the 'New Inn', to take away bricks and return with coal and deal. In 1964 the village protested strongly when the Yare Commission reopened the southern dyke because they said hire boats would destroy the living of the four reed cutters on Rockland and bring in the worst type of 'marsh cowboy' wildfowler. In 1981 the head of Rockland dyke was dredged out wider for the hire boats, but remained in the ownership of the local Poors Trust.

21. Brooms of Brundall. The Norfolk Broads Yachting Company opened a boatyard in 1898 and later sold it to their manager C.J.Broom. Three generations later the Brooms had become Britain's longest established power boat builders and had a hire fleet of fifty boats. The marina was dug out in the 1970s and in 1989 the adjoining boatyard of Colin Chapman's Moonraker factory was acquired.

22. On a really high tide salt water will get up to Brundall.

23. Surlingham Ferry. This horse ferry to Brundall closed in 1943. The Victorian writer G.Christopher Davies complained bitterly that the Yare above Buckenham was silted.

24. Postwick, pronounced Pos'ick, once had a wherry staithe up a short dyke. In Victorian times people from Yarmouth used to come up by steamer and pleasure boat to picnic on Postwick Hill.

25. Kirby Bedon Staithe was used in the eighteenth century, but by 1996 the long dyke up to it had silted up. There was a walk way from Kirby Bedon Staithe up the dyke to Bramerton Wood End where the wherrymen were fond of stopping to wait for the tide to turn in their favour.

26. Wharf used for loading sugar beet.

27. The Yare Amateur Rowing Club used to be on the site which became the car park. On the up steam bend in the river was the staithe where wherries loaded marl from the pit behind the ruins of Whitlingham Church. The Colmans used the dyke to keep their boats in before World War I.

28. In the nineteenth century James Hobrough & Son operated their dredgers from The Dockyard below the 'Griffen'. These were used to keep the Broads rivers clear. In 1940 the business was sold to May Gurney.

29. In 1868 Stephen Fields moved his boat building business from the Ferry Yard, Norwich to Thorpe. This yard was sold in 1894 when he died.

30. New Cut dug in 1844 when the railway line was built. This channel allowed ships to continue to get up to Norwich.

31. About 1989 gravel was dug on the marshes for the Norwich Southern By-Pass and this resulted in three new broads being created beside the New Cut.

32. Site of the Norwich Rowing Club is called Trowse Hythe, but the Hythe at Trowse used by wherries was further up stream where the road runs beside the river. The wherries came to the Hythe in the nineteenth century to load marl from the pit just up the road. The Hythe Cottage is now called Yare Cottage. Hythe is the Saxon name for a quay. The River Tass just up stream was straightened between 1889 and 1906.

33. May Gurney operated part of their dredging business from a yard at Trowse. This yard was between the Yare and Tass backing on to the point where the two rivers met.

34 . The commercial port of Norwich moved down to the King's Street area in the 12th century.

35. Towers which were part of the fourteenth century wall for protecting Norwich. Carrow towers had a strong Spanish iron chain which could be placed across the river to act as a boom to prevent raiding ships going up. In the nineteenth century one tower was used as a coke oven to supply the nearby maltings.

36. The Foundry Bridge was built in 1844 and rebuilt in 1886 with iron made in the city.

37. Bishops Bridge. Possible site of a Roman ford. First bridge here before 1269. Present bridge built about 1340 and is the only surviving medieval bridge in Norwich. Wherries often had difficulties getting under the bridge. To get them down deeper in the water they used to invite local people aboard for extra weight.

38. The Great Hospital, Bishopsgate had, a swan pit, until about 1914 in which cygnets caught on the Yare were fattened up to eat for Christmas.

39. The Saxon port of Norwich was probably between Whitefriars and Fye Bridges. Excavations have shown that near St Martin-at-Palace Plain there was a gravel spit on which bush wood had been laid. Persumably so that long ships could be beached here and unloaded.

40. Fye Bridge. In the medieval period an oak causeway was laid across the river here.

41. Just below the Anchor Wharf bridge, two of the wherry posts have survived. Wherries coming up the Wensum were always going against the current because the water from New Mills went over the top of a flood tide. There was a series of posts from Trowse Eye to the New Mills so that wherries could be hauled up.

42. New Mills got their names from the watermill built in 1430. Although the keels and wherries had great difficulty going up the narrow river above Bishop's Bridge they did get as far as the New Mills. In the early nineteenth century 30ft flat bottomed spritsail barges operated just above the New Mills carrying trees to timber mills at Taverham.

Chapter Three

NORTHERN WATERS

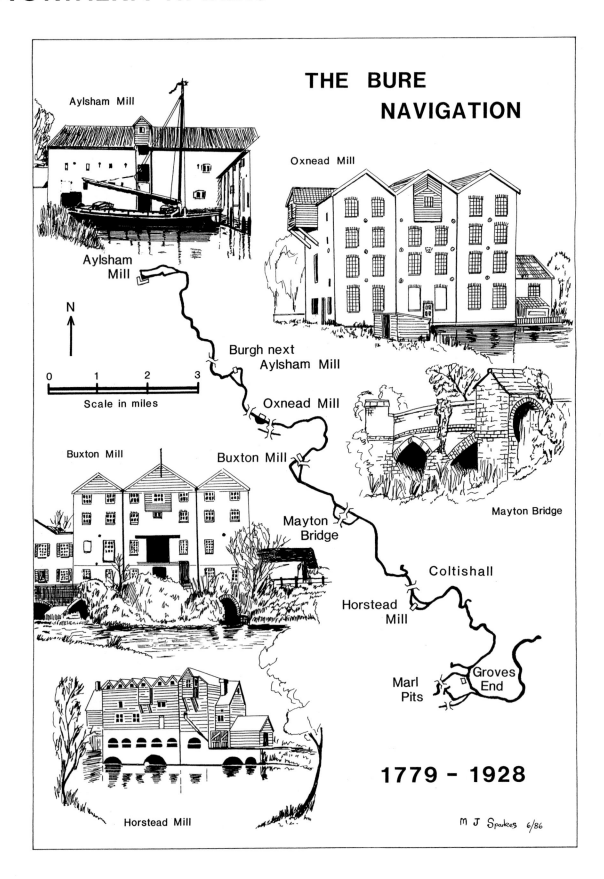

Aylsham Mill

THE BURE NAVIGATION

Oxnead Mill

Aylsham Mill

N

0   1   2   3
Scale in miles

Burgh next Aylsham Mill

Oxnead Mill

Buxton Mill

Buxton Mill

Mayton Bridge

Mayton Bridge

Coltishall

Horstead Mill

Marl Pits

Groves End

1779 - 1928

M J Sparkes 6/86

Horstead Mill

60. Looking down from Wroxham Bridge in about 1908. Wherries that started off in trade were sometimes converted for holiday hire. On the left is the *Britannia* which had a small transom stern, then *Widgeon* and the *John & Henry* under sail.

The shed on the left had been built for the Norfolk Broads Yacht Co. The Norfolk Broads Yacht yard was later sold to their manager Alfred Pegg and then to the Collins'. In 1914 Hobrough started to dredge dykes out in the marsh below for the expanding hire boat fleet. They enlarged the tiny 'pulk' (pond), Daisy Broad, but work was stopped by World War I. After this war the men returned and the whole marsh was dug out into dykes for the hire boat stations.

61. Two wherries racing on Wroxham Broad about 1902. The leading wherry has a white 'snout' painted on the bow. This practice started because the wherries did not carry lights at night. The wherry astern appears to have been a very old craft even then because she has a slopping bow and a very square cut sail. It is said that as the trees grew up on the Broads the peak of the wherry's sails were cut higher.

62. Two pleasure wherries and a power boat on Wroxham Broad in about 1925. The power boat is a Brooke Baby class.

63. Fred, Joe and Jim crew of the Norfolk Broads hire yacht *Iantly* in 1893. The first recorded holiday on the Broads was of a voyage made on a lateen rigged cutter with two paid hands in 1840, but the writer seemed to think that hiring was perfectly normal so it must have been going on before this.

64. The cabin of the hire yacht *Iantly* in 1893. The Victorian hirers only visited at the height of the summer. Early Broads hire boats, or wherry or yacht, were hired out with a paid crew. Only in the 1920s did self drive hire boats begin to make up most of the hire fleets.

65. The 43ft Broads yacht *America* was built by Ernest Collins at Wroxham and appeared in the first Blake hire fleet catalogue in 1908. She was hired out with a skipper and remained in the catalogue until 1947 when it is thought she was sailed to the West Indies.

In 1993 Mike Barnes was looking for a classic Broads yacht to produce in fibre glass to add to the Norfolk Broads Yacht Co fleet of hire yachts. He asked Landamores if they could re-create the *America* hull shape from old photographs. The result was the new 37ft *America* launched at St Olaves in 1994.

The Collins' at Wroxham were the leading Broads builders until Herbert Woods took over his father's Potter

Heigham boat yard and produced the 29ft *Moonraker* in 1930. She was the first Broads yacht to have the bermudian rig. He continued with the double ended *Ladybird* in 1935 and then *Evening Flight*. Fifty years after they were built they were regarded as being some of the fastest yachts on the Broads.

66. A party of gentlemen aboard the pleasure wherry *Five Brothers* about 1905.

Many people came to the Broads after reading Christopher Davies *Handbook to the Rivers and Broads of Norfolk and Suffolk* which first appeared in 1882 and ran to many editions. The following year a railway guide came out telling people in the Midlands and London how to reach the Norfolk Broads and what to find when they got there. The Great Eastern Railway very actively promoted holidays on the Broads and commissioned John Payne Jennings to take a series of photographs to go in their railway carriages. Payne Jennings also published his *Sun Pictures of the Norfolk Broads* in 1891 and since this there has been a steady stream of books about the area.

67. A wherry, fitted with a cabin for summer hiring, passing an eel fishers hut on the River Bure about 1910.

There were yachts and pleasure barges on the Norfolk rivers in the eighteenth century and around the 1840s wherries were being hired for summer cruising. These early pleasure wherries only had basic accommodation and for the rest of the year they carried cargoes. By around 1885 owners were fitting cabins and white sails on wherries and the holiday demand was such that they did not return to cargo carrying. After this a few pleasure wherries were built for private owners or for hiring out.

Some hirers did not want to hire a common working wherry so wherry yachts evolved. These usually had carvel hulls with long elegant counter sterns for the passengers to sit on. First of these was probably the *Kiama* in 1876, but it was not until the Edwardian era that they became really popular. About fifteen were built on the Bure.

The wherry skippers used to think it was promotion to take over a wherry yacht although it was more uncomfortable because they lived forward, not aft, in the pleasure wherry's cuddy.

68. The pleasure wherry *Solace* sailing in front of the wherry *Albion* at the '75 Birthday Party' of *Olive* on Wroxham Broad in 1984. The wherry yacht *Lady Edith (Norada)* was also there and this was the first time so many members of the wherry family had sailed together for over thirty years .

The 59ft *Solace* was built by Daniel Hall at Reedham in 1903 for Commander Rogers of Ingham Hall. She is still sailed without an engine but has a launch built by Percy Collins in 1924 for towing her around in calms.

69. The Broads yacht *Water Lily* taking part in Horning Regatta about 1909. Just behind her are the swings of the fair that accompanied the Regatta. Horning Regatta started 1903.

41

70. Meal time on the houseboat *Cleopatra* at Horning in about 1925. Mr H. Mills, a Huddersfield solicitor, was a good draughtsman and designed the Egyptian motifs on the side of his *Cleopatra* which was built by Arthur Powley at Horning. This houseboat ended up as a floating store at Southgates yard and was lost in a disastrous fire in 1939.

71. Another family group on the *Cleopatra* at Horning about 1925.

72. The lifeboat *Friend of All Nations* at Horning about 1925 with Mr H. Mill's houseboat *Cleopatra* in the background.

The 43ft *Friend of All Nations* was one of several beach yolls and lifeboats which finished up on the Broads as motor boats or houseboats. She was built by James Critten at Southtown, Yarmouth in 1863 as a private lifeboat for the Young Fliers beach company at Gorleston. The beach companies rescue work was mainly based on small sailing ships getting into difficulties.

73. The trial trip on the *Friend of All Nations*. She later became a motor cruiser in the Eastick hire fleet. In 1979 she was bought by David Collier and used as a private cruiser based at Wroxham. By 1996 she was the oldest craft afloat in Norfolk, but not the only lifeboat. There was also the 47ft *Elizabeth Simpson* which was built by Beeching Brothers at Yarmouth in 1889. The Gorleston Volunteer Lifeboat Association used her to save 400 lives before 1939. She became a tripper boat, first at Yarmouth and then at Potter Heigham where she was laid up in 1996.

74. The drainage mill and a wherry yacht with a bold sheer at Horning about 1909. Gedge built up the marsh in the foreground using mud dredged from the river which had previously been dried off on the bank for two years. The whole area above the 'Ferry Boat' has had several dykes cut into it and houses built round them.

75. The 'Ferry Boat Inn', Horning in about 1935 with the floating pontoon 'horse ferry' on the left. The wherry yacht is the *Goldfinch* built in 1910 by Alfred Collins.

76. The wherry *Edith* at Ludham Bridge in about 1905. This scene is typical of the wherry era when there were few trees around the Norfolk rivers, either the cattle ate them or wherrymen cut them down. The open Broads were all very much larger and have steadily decreased in size.

77. The last of the cargo wherries, *Lord Roberts* at Ludham Bridge in about 1968. The motorised *Lord Roberts* was then being used for Broads maintenance . The mast was used when driving posts in on Breydon Water.

The *Lord Roberts*, *I'll Try, Fir* and *Dispatch* were all trading with sails until the late 1930s. The wherry *Hilda* was trading with sail only until 1940, but the Wherry Trust bought the *Albion* in 1949 and put her back in trade under sail until 1953. In 1950 May,Gurney had thirteen motor wherries, mostly loading from dredgers in the summer and sugar beeting in the winter. P.'Blucher' Thain of Potter Heigham had a number of these motor wherries carrying sugar beet from Repps and Potter Heigham to Cantley. There were a few other freights, but when there was no work the wherrymen worked on the farms. At the end of the 1964-65 sugar beet campaign the factory stopped taking beet by water and many wherries were taken straight away to be sunk as bank supports.

The *Lord Roberts* took her last freight in 1969 when she carried timber for the walk ways from Wroxham down to the Hoveton Nature Reserve. She was given to the Norfolk Wherry Trust, but their policy of just keeping one wherry sailing meant she was not rebuilt.

78. A wherry sailing up the Ant past How Hill Staithe about 1922. She is towing her slip keel along side so that she is probably bound up to North Walsham.

45

79. Reed cutter on the Ant in 1950.

80. Barton Staithe about 1891. It is said that before the trees grew up around Barton a man could stand above the staithe and see the open sea.

　　The dyke in the foreground went up to Cox's slipway and beyond that the little store used for coal brought up by wherries from Yarmouth. In the background is a yacht and behind her a sunken wherry.

Above. 81. The 23ft lateener *Maria* on Barton Broad around 1860. It is believed that the lateen rig was introduced to the Broads by an army officer who had served at Malta. Certainly in the 1820s this eastern rig was adopted for racing on the Broads and continued to be popular until the 1870s when the cutters took over. The *Maria* was built at Yarmouth in 1827 and was regarded as being the fastest yacht on the Broads until she stopped racing in 1914. In 1969 John Perryman and C. Thrower discovered the *Maria* in a thatched boathouse near Callow Green, Barton Turf and she was taken to the Maritime Museum for East Anglia at Yarmouth.

82. The lateener *Britannia*, a half size version of the *Maria*, sailing at Barton in 1972. She is not nearly as beautiful as the original 'Black' *Maria* which is a most handsome gentleman's yacht. When tacking a lateener against the wind the yard was pulled round the mast by a tacking line. The *Britannia* did not fit in with the Norfolk Wherry Trust's programme and in 1995 was being used by Peter Bower as a tender for *Hathor*. He fitted her with an electric engine, but found that with plenty of ballast she sailed very well.

83. The 1936 wherry race on Barton Broad. The wherry on the right which has just broken her gaff is the *Hilda*. There was a whip round after the race which raised £3 to pay for the repair. Ahead of *Hilda* is *Dispatch* and then the mast of the pleasure wherry *Solace* and the winner *Cornucopia* is on the very left.

In the eighteenth century Water Frolics were held on most Broads, but by the 1870s these were replaced by regattas in which the wherry race was the main event. The main wherry races were at Barton, Oulton Broad, Wroxham and Burgh Castle and there were also races at sea off Yarmouth and Lowestoft. World War I seems to have stopped most the wherry races, but Barton restarted and sailed between 1924-37.

84. The 1936 Barton Wherry Race just after the *Hilda* has lowered her sail and passed the pleasure wherry *Solace* on the right rhond (bank). The *Ella* has just passed *Hilda* and ahead of her is *Dispatch* while the *Cornucopia* is romping way ahead. After starting with their mud weights down, wherries went twice round the course. *Cornucopia* won in two hours fifty minutes.

Just forward of the bow of the *Solace* on the right can be seen the floating club house. Barton Broad yachtsmen always considered themselves real sailors because they had to sail to reach their club house.

48

85. The 22ft Norfolk punts racing on Barton Broad about 1936. The Norfolk punts were originally used by wildfowlers to shoot duck during the winter. They had 2-bore punt guns mounted on their fore decks. The punts were either rowed between shots or 'shoved' with a quant. They also carried a lug sail or spritsail and were raced in the summer regattas. There was a punt race on Hickling Broad in 1923 and in 1936 the Norfolk Punt Club was formed on Barton Broad.

After World War II Dr Basil Tracey revived the Norfolk Punt Club. Members had been racing on Wroxham Broad but the club returned to Barton. The punts then developed into high performance racing dinghies of a plywood or fibreglass construction. The class rules were rewritten in 1986 to spur on development.

86. Stalham Staithe in 1928. There were already hire craft at the staithe, but after World War II the meadows in the background were dredged out to create the hire craft marinas.

87. Stalham Yacht Station about 1935.

88. A wherry at Wayford Bridge in about 1900 with the cottage in the background where the wherryman lived. This wherry was built by Allen of Coltishall and owned by Hewitt the Wayford malster.

The wherries had lost some of their coal carrying work to the railways, but villages without a railway station still found it cheaper to have their coal delivered by wherry. In 1887 the wherry *Emily* of Hickling, owned by George Beales the landlord of the 'Pleasure Boat', was taking a freight of beans, wheat or hay down to Yarmouth one week, and coming back with coal, brought in by sea, the next. She loaded about 16 tons and was typical of the wherries working to the rural hinterland which lasted until lorries began to take over country haulage in the early 1920s.

Above. 89. The transom sterned wherry *Elizabeth* and another wherry at the Wayford Malt Houses around 1900.

These buildings belong to the wherry age. The red brick cottages and pan tile rooves were often built between about 1770-1830 while black tarred weather boarding was being built right up until corrugated iron became popular after about 1910.

90. Two wherries approaching the Honing lock on the North Walsham canal about 1900. The wherrymen spent a great deal of time in the narrow rivers pushing their craft along with 24ft quants. The wherries which traded into the northern rivers generally carried 20-30 tons while those on the Norwich River loaded 35-40 tons.

This section of the the canal was dug about 1775, but the original course of the Ant bent to the west round into Dilham Lake. In the 1830s wherries were still sailing up Dilham Lake to load at the water mill at the southern end. However Dilham Lake slowly grew over with reeds so that by 1885 it was no longer open water. By 1996 the site of Dilham Lake was a low meadow, Honing Lock was still there although the lock gates had long since gone.

THE NORTH WALSHAM
& DILHAM CANAL

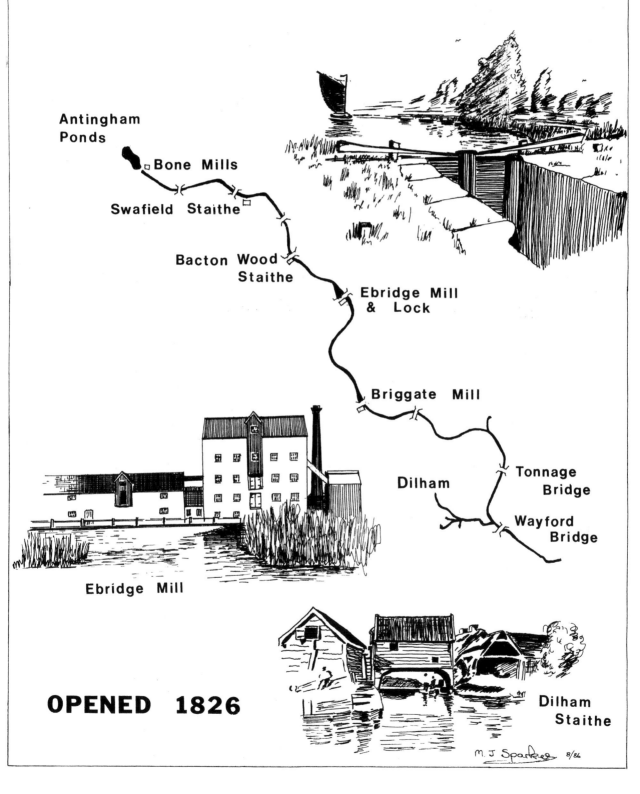

Antingham
Ponds

Bone Mills

Swafield Staithe

Bacton Wood
Staithe

Ebridge Mill
& Lock

Briggate Mill

Dilham

Tonnage
Bridge

Wayford
Bridge

Ebridge Mill

Dilham
Staithe

m. J. Sparkes 8/86

OPENED 1826

92. A wherry at Spa Common on the North Walsham and Dilham Navigation in about 1925. A canal was dug out beside the River Ant in 1826 which allowed wherries to get right up to Antingham Ponds. This was the most northerly point of navigation on the Broads rivers.

Opposite Top. 93. Part of the North Walsham and Dilham Navigation at Royston road about 1920. This navigation was not a commercial success because it had not been completed long when the railways reached Norfolk.

Opposite Bottom. 94. Men loading 'shoofs' of reed into a reed lighter in 1887. This is one of the many famous Broads photographs taken by P.H.Emerson. Reeds were cut around the Broads during the winter and brought back to a staithe in double ended clinker punts known as load boats or reed lighters. These Norfolk boats had very little draft and a wide beam so that they could carry a large load in shallow water. The large 'load' boat was over 20ft long and could carry 600 'shoofs' (sheaves) of reeds. There were smaller 'half load' boats and even 'quarter load' boats.

The pointed stern reed lighters were very beautiful craft, but they were not practical once engines came in because of the problems of the prop shaft going through the stern posts. In the 1980s, however, a reed lighter was built to transport reed and people on the How Hill Estate. In 1991 the Norfolk Naturalists Trust had the 19ft reed lighter *Billy Nudd* built as a runabout and in 1995 the Broads Authority had the 23ft *Helen of Ranworth* built by Paul Brown with an electric engine to act as a ferry at Ranworth

95. A Broads yacht on South Walsham Broad in 1906. There appears to be a paid hand on the fordeck and the hirers wife aft.

96. A wherry fitted with a cabin for summer hirers, with an early motor cruiser alongside, at South Walsham staithe about 1908.

97. The 43ft *Madie* helmed by her owner Reg Parsons of the Thurne 'Lion' at Thurne Mouth in 1981. The following year she was rigged out again with the Broad's gaff cutter rig after being a bermudian yacht for over thirty years. Built in 1904 by Ernest Collins at Wroxham the *Madie* was one of the Broads A Class, usually known as the 'big class'. After eighty years of hard racing *Madie's* hull was badly hogged. She was bought by Mike Barnes and totally rebuilt in 1986. With the *Sparklet* built by Bunn at Wroxham in 1905, she was the last of the Victorian and Edwardian gentleman's day racers still sailing in 1995.

98. The 34ft *Evening Flight* racing at Thurne Mouth about 1982. At this time she was considered one of the fastest yachts on the Broads with the *Madie, Raisena, Ladybird* and *White Wings*.

99. Acle Regatta in about 1984. Left to right 27ft *Pippa*, 43ft *Madie*, 29ft *Moonraker*, *Halycon* behind and the 28ft *Melinda* which was racing for the first time. Racing on the Broads was very popular in the Edwardian period and after this motor craft became popular. Racing continued, but in the 1960s the hire fleet operators started to sell off their wooden sailing craft. This brought more back into private ownership which stimulated racing again. Following this there was great enthusiasm for restoring Broads yachts.

By 1982 new yachts started appearing. The 33ft *Cirrus,* the West-style hull, Andrew Wolstenholme-design, was launched. Also Easticks of Acle built the *Woodpecker,* the first Broads sailing yacht to be built in fibreglass and the first of the Eastick 28 Class. Other fibreglass classes followed on and A. Landamore's 28ft class proved very fast. Andrew Wolstenholme designed 25ft and 30ft classes based on *Sparklet*. Following this came the 22ft Bure Class built by Paul Reynolds at Upton and fitted out by Colin Buttifant.

100. Racing at Thurne Mouth about 1983 with the 'White Boat' 66 in the foreground. The 'White Boat' is the general name given to the Yare and Bure One Design half decked day racer. The other long established day racer is the Broads One Design known as the 'Brown Boat' because of the varnished mahogany hull. This class was designed by Linton Hope and they first raced in 1901. Both White Boat and Brown Boat classes have been continued in fibreglass, although the new Brown Boats sometimes have different coloured hulls.

101. The Norfolk Wherry Trust's *Albion* at their new headquarters at Womack Water, Ludham in 1984, the year the Trust had the dyke cut. The new boathouse followed in 1988.

102. Vincent Pargeter in 1981 standing on the bow of the 60ft wherry *Maud* just after she had been raised from Ranworth Broad. She was taken from here to Upton Dyke for the start of her fifteen year rebuild.

The *Maud* was built by Daniel Hall at Reedham in 1899 for Walter Bunn of Yarmouth. In 1918 the *Maud* was sold to J.S.Hobrough who used her and many other wherries for transporting mud dredged from the rivers. In 1940 this firm was sold to May Gurney of Trowse and as the old wherries wore out they were sunk along the banks to prevent erosion. This was the *Maud's* fate at Ranworth in about 1965.

103. Regatta day at Potter Heigham about 1930.

104. A Broads lugger passing Potter Heigham, pronounced Potter Hey'em, in about 1913. This type of lugger was very popular for racing in the Edwardian era and on the Broads they were almost a development of the lateener.

The shed in the background is the Herbert Woods No 2 Shed which was built by the Norfolk Broads Yachting Co. In 1950 Woods owned George Applegates boatyard which had sheds between the bridges and on the south side of the road bridge.

Norfolk Broads — Potter Heigham

105. P.E. Thain's wherry *I'll Try* at Potter Heigham shortly before she sank in 1964.

106. The 'Pleasure Boat' Inn at Hickling about 1900. The reed 'load boat' in the dyke has an extra plank 'rose up on' on her sides which could mean that she had been used for dredging.

This was how the 'Pleasure Boat' staithe looked in 1890 when E.H.Emerson set out from here in his wherry *Maid of the Mist* to spend a year sailing and photographing the Broads. Emerson approached his voyage round the Broads like an explorer entering a new country. He was keen to record the old way of life of wherrymen, marsh farmers and reed cutters before it was swept aside by the holiday trade.

107. A gang of marsh mowers cutting the sedge on the marsh just north of Whiteslea, Hickling Broad in 1934. This was done to improve the wildfowl shooting. From left to right Charlie Gibbs, 'Nodger' Amies, Mike Nudd, James Forsythe, Edwin Vincent, Hedell Bell, Ted Piggen and Roy Nudd. The best mower went at the end of the line to keep the work straight.

108. Hickling marsh mowing gang 1934. Left to right 'Nodger' Amies, Charlie Gibbs, Hedell Bell, Mike Nudd, Edwin Vincent, Roy Nudd, Ted Piggen and Jim Vincent.

109. How Hill Marshman Eric Edwards proudly demonstrating dressing Norfolk reed to Sir Derek Barber, chairman of the Countryside Commission at an event in 1989 to celebrate the starting of the Broads Authority.

110. Jim Vincent, head keeper to Lord Desborough, in a gun punt on Hickling Broad in 1933 The Hickling punts had round bottoms while the Breydon punts were flat bottomed. These punts also had a lug sail.

Twice every January the Hickling Broad coot shoots took place. The gentry and sometimes royalty stayed at Whiteslea Lodge and up to 20 punts and boats, each quanted by a marsh man with 'the gun' sitting amidships, left the 'Pleasure Boat' staithe and went to the eastern end of the Broad. The beaters and guns on the shore prevented the coot from flying away and then the line of boats move up the Broad slowly. The coot were then shot, often in large numbers, as they flew back to the other end of the Broad over the heads of the guns. After Lord Desborough's death the Norfolk Naturalists acquired most of Hickling Broad and rented the rest. Sedge was sold and the shooting let out to pay for the rented area. In 1964 duck and coot shooting ended on Hickling.

111. Hickling Broad about 1935. To the left is the dyke leading up to the 'Pleasure Boat' Inn while the dyke to the right was used for unloading reeds and only about 20ft of this remained in 1995.

About 1934 'Nodger' Amies and James Forsythe were quanting a half load boat back across Hickling on a breezey day when she filled and sank. They sat on top of the reeds and shouted to Charlie Gibbs, who was in a full load boat in front. Fortunately he came back and rescued them. They returned the next day and raised the boat.

HICKLING BROAD. (506)

112. West Somerton road in February, 1938 after an on-shore gale and very high tide flattened the sand dunes at Horsey and the sea flooded inland as far as the Meadow Dike.

James Forsythe was staying at Scratby Hall and went over to Hickling to borrow a punt from Jim Vincent to go bird watching. He was told that there had been a massive sea flood so he set off in the punt to investigate. He went down to the Meadow Dike across Horsey Mere and up to the Staithe. Here he discovered the sea had flooded all the marshes. In the punt he went to the pub at Horsey to find water up to the top of the bar and the place abandoned. From here he punted out to the gap at the old mouth of the Hundred Stream. Going south he passed this Austin Seven car abandoned on the road. The driver had been rescued by Herbert Woods in a motor boat and 'werry near crazy he wor' when they took him off. This extraordinary voyage ended by going to Somerton Staithe where he found the river and returned by Martham Broad, Candle Dyke across Heigham Sound and back to Whiteslea.

The Hundred Steam is the old mouth of the River Thurne which was closed off from the sea in about 1350. Local folk legend recalled ships riding at anchor where cattle now graze. The sea had flooded Horsey area via the Hundred Stream in 1607, 1791 and 1938. The area was again flooded in 1953 although that time the sea broke through the Marram Hills at Sea Palling.

113. Farm workers bringing the live stock back from Ford's Farm, Horsey after the 1938 floods. These floods seem to have been the worst since 1791 when the sea swept away much of village of Waxham Pava and flooded inland.

114. A floating chicken hut at Somerton after the 1938 floods. This type of scene has haunted eastern Norfolk down the centuries.

In a small highly populated country such as England space is one of our most precious assets and to loose any land is a disaster. In the twentieth century sea defences have been successful and stopped major coastal erosion. It is absolutely neccessary to continue the fight to prevent the sea from tearing away the land. Unchecked, the sea would take out all the Norfolk coastal villages and flood through into the Broads . In the early 1990s rock islands were built off Sea Palling to combat the tremendous power of the waves.

115. The Norfolk Wherry Trust's *Albion* being quanted away from Horsey Staithe in 1989. The *Albion* is rather large for the northern waters and a great deal of hard work is needed to quant her out of tight corners.

116. The Norfolk Dumpling Class dinghies racing in the Yare and Bure Regatta at Acle on July 9 1909.

117. Norfolk Broads luggers at a regatta at Acle about 1912.

118. Eastick's hire pleasure wherry *Red Rover* near Acle about 1930.

119. Peter Bower sailing the 56ft pleasure wherry *Hathor* down the River Bure in 1995 with the wherry yacht *Norada* and Stracey Arms Mill in the background. Peter Bower started charter work with the *Olive* in 1977 and with Barney Matthews he formed the Wherry Yacht Charter which operates *Olive*, *Norada* and *Hathor* from Wroxham.

The *Hathor* was built by Daniel Hall at Reedham for Ethel and Helen Colman in 1905. Their brother Alan had died in Egypt after going on a trip on the Nile at Luxor on a river boat called *Hathor* so the Misses Colmans gave their wherry the same name in his memory. This pleasure wherry was sailed on the Broads for years with the Colman and Boardman families aboard. She survived World War II in her boat house, but in about 1964 she became a house boat at Wroxham until Wherry Yacht Charters purchased her in 1985 and started sailing her again. The *Norada* also spent World War II in a boat shed, but *Olive* was moored on Wroxham Broad and people had holidays on her.

Opposite Top. 120. The 53ft wherry yacht *Norada* going down the Bure on the ebb tide passing the 'Ferry Inn', Stokesby in 1995.

The *Norada* was built by Ernest Collins in 1912 and was hired out with a skipper and steward until 1950 when this became too expensive. In 1964 she was bought by Barney Matthews, who had been a skipper with Collins, and she was extensively rebuilt to sailing order.

Opposite Bottom. 121. The wherry *Dispatch* leaving Yarmouth bound north in the River Bure in 1936. Her crew are father and son Rump. In recent times the crew of a wherry have been called skipper and mate, but the old practice was to call them wherryman and waterman.

The *Dispatch* had a small engine fitted, but it was hardly big enough to push her along. She was trading under motor and sail until being damaged by German bombs while she was at Read's Mill, Norwich in 1942.

122. The foot Suspension Bridge over the Bure linking Yarmouth with Runwell in about 1905. On the right near the North West Tower are wherries discharging while on the left are two shrimpers.

Just down river from here the Bure flows into Yarmouth Harbour. This was the Cape Horn of the Norfolk rivers. Wherries coming down the Bure under sail had to time their passage to leave the Bure on the last of the ebb and catch the first of the flood tide going up to Breydon Water. Wherries going down the Harbour used to drop their mud weights and then drift stern first down under the bridge. If there was a misjudgement and they hit the bridge the force of the tide sometimes rolled them over and sank them.

GORLESTON LIFEBOAT

122a. Gorleston Lifeboat. The Norfolk and Suffolk Lifeboats were a development of the beach yawls.

70

RIVERS BURE, ANT AND THURNE

RIVER BURE

1. Caister on Sea. Roman trading town which guarded the old entrance to the Norfolk rivers.

2. Caistor Castle was built 1432-35 by Sir John Falstolf. The bricks were made two miles away and brought up Pickerill Holme and through a cut to a barge dock under the tower.

3. Mautby Swim. Before World War I cattle were swum across the river to reach the grazing on Halvergate marshes.

4. Runham Swim. Place where cattle were swum across the river.

5. Stracey Arms Mill was built in 1831 on a raft of pitch pine with 40ft piles beneath it. This was the time the new road was built through to Yarmouth. There were eleven windmills below Acle pumping water from the Halvergate Marshes. Stracey Mill was worked by the Aurnp family from the time it was built until it closed in 1931. In 1967 Lady Stracey gave the mill to Norfolk County Council for preservation. An electric pump replaced the mill and used in times of flooding, but by 1995 the water was mostly allowed to run back from the Bure on to Halvergate for the cattle. The water level is kept down by a pump on the Breydon side.

6. Stokesby horse ferry stopped about 1911.

7. The dyke up to Tunstall appears to have been dug out about 1760 and was used by wherries. The last one trading up here was *Tunstall Trader* until about 1914.

8. Acle Bridge. Because of the narrow bends at the lower end the Bure most of northern waters are fresh water, but a really big tide will push salt water up to Acle Bridge.

9. Dyke for wherries up to Upton was there in 1796. Oby windmill, a brick pump mill built in 1753, can be seen across the marshes and the river.

10. In the 1950s the Bure below St Benet's was dredged of 'marl', river mud, which was taken by motor wherry and put on the rhonds in the Thurne.

11. St Benet's at Holme Abbey. Probably founded about 1020 when King Canute gave the land south of Ludham to the Abbey. Viking raiders destroyed the monastery in the nineth century, but it was rebuilt and became very rich on the profits of turf digging because it acquired the rights to dig in most of the adjoining villages. The Abbey was originally linked by a causeway to Horning Hall and in the eighteenth century it was still possible to see the remains of a timber bridge. Only the Abbey gatehouse remains but in the nineteenth century there was a windmill grinding oilseed in the Abbey ruins. Top of the windmill was blown off in 1863. The dock for the medieval Abbey was directly opposite South Walsham dyke.

12. In the Victorian times the 'Chequers' Inn was a wherryman's pub on the north bank. The landlord J.J.Dawson Paul operated a steam boat which towed wherries through this difficult reach. The inn became a marsh farmer's cottage but was burnt down in 1886.

13. Ward Marsh, part of the parish of Horning. At some period the Bure channel was straightened creating Ward Marsh. This was still an island in about 1905 but the channel became overgrown.

14. Fleet Dike connecting south Walsham Broad to old Bure channel was probably dug in the medieval period. The old East Anglian word fleet means shallow.

15. The inner South Walsham Broad was closed by the landowner with post and chains in 1901. This resulted in the village people sailing in force and re-entering the Broad. A compromise was reached whereby the public had the right to navigate on the Broad but it remained private property with no mooring, fishing or swimming allowed. The outer Broad remained the parish staithe, but by 1994 was only open to residents. Jones Staithe just above the Parish Staithe had a granary where wherries discharged.

16. Ranworth Broad is closed to navigation. In 1949 Col Henry Cator gave Ranworth and Cockshoot Broad to the Norfolk Naturalists' Trust and they closed off Ranworth for conservation. Cockshoot Broad was almost completely overgrown, when in 1981 it was dredged out, but was not opened to boats. This area was kept as part of English Nature's Bure Marshes reserve which runs from Ranworth Broad right up river to Hudson's Bay.

17. Under the Enclosure Act, Horning people retained 30 acres on which they had the right to cut 30000 turfs for fuel every year. Until about 1930 Horning and Woodbastwick people were cutting turf for their household fires.

18. In 1949 Herbert Woods led a fleet of craft on to Little Hoveton Broad after the land owner had blocked the entrance. The end of this bitter dispute was that the High Court ruled that the public had a right to navigate on the Broad although the bed belonged to the landowner. Because the Broads started as medieval peat diggings the bottom of all the Broads were privately owned.

19. Ferry Inn, Horning was hit by a bomb which killed 15 people in 1941. The bombing also destroyed the chain ferry which had been operated by Fred Cook. After this a smaller boat continued as a ferry until about 1968. In 1993 Colin Facey Boats restarted the ferry to Woodbastwick with the *Stanley Arthur* named after Mr Facey's father.

20. Colin Facey took over Turner' yard in about 1983. In the early 1990s there was considerable redevelopement for the holiday trade in this area.

21. H.T.Percival started a boatyard here in about 1929. During World War II these yacht builders built MTBs and other fast naval craft. To allow them to get under the bridges these craft were not fitted with deck structures until they reached Yarmouth.

22. The green in the middle of Lower Street on the river side is the site of the Horning malt house which was pulled down in 1934. It is believed that ships biscuits were produced here during the Crimean War.

23. Original 'Swan Inn' was a typical eighteenth century Norfolk red brick house. This area was known to wherrymen as the 'Cinder Ovens' named after a coke producing oven which was on the Woodbastwick side. The 'Swan' was rebuilt in 1897 for the rapidly increasing holiday trade and enlarged again in the Edwardian period. On the bend at the up stream end of Town Reach there was a large wooden mill until about 1910.

24. The Black Horse Staithe in Little Hoveton Broad was used by wherries.

25. The wherries used a short cut through a dyke called The Dam, and then crossed Great Hoveton Broad to Hudson Bay and back into the Bure. These broads were still just open to navigation in the 1890s. In the 1960s a Nature Trail was set up with agreement of the owner T.C.R.Blofield.

26. Ernest Collins and Sons boat yard at Wroxham. Robert Collins had moved here from Coltishall in 1886 and he built up one of the early hire fleets.

27. Alfred Collins boat yard 1910, Wroxham. The last of the sheds from the former Collins yard was pulled down in 1995.

28. Next to the bridge on the Wroxham bank was John Loynes yard. He moved here from Norwich in 1878 because he found most of the people who hired his boats preferred the north river. John's son Sidney joined in the firm in 1910 and was a keen racing man. More recently Broads Tours have become based here.

29. Just down stream of the road bridge on the Hoveton side there was a maltings and a public staithe although the area has now been developed for tourism.

30. Above the bridge on the Wroxham side was Ambrose Thrower's yard. He started as a blacksmith and hired out steam launches in the Edwardian period.

31. For 34 years George 'Nobby' Cox had an eel sett above the railway bridge until 1936 when he fell in and was drowned.

32. Horstead Marl Hole. From the sixteenth century until the pits closed in 1870 wherries came into this system of canals to load marl which was taken and spread on the fields to improve the soil structure. Very small 12 ton wherries were used to bring the chalk away from the pits and in one place there was a tunnel going half a mile into the hill side. After the pits closed the whole area was planted up with fir trees and the Victorians called it Little Switzerland.

33. Belaugh parish and church staithe. Kerrison and Press had yards at Belaugh and the wherry *Friendship* was owned here in 1795.

34. Anchor Street boatyard probably used in the 1500s when there was keel traffic going up to Aylsham. In 1864 Allen bought this yard at Coltishall for £400. Allens built the small 20 ton wherries which were used on the North River. They were building one wherry a year until 1900. In 1912 they built the last trading wherry, *Ella*. Before the family sold the yard in 1974 Clifford Allen operated a hire fleet here and on the River Shannon. The yard later became a housing estate.

35. There were malt houses at Coltishall in the eighteenth century and by l900 there were nineteen malt houses in the village. In 1926 malting finished here and the malt house beside the 'Rising Sun' was closed and pulled down about a decade later.

36. On the south channel is the site of Horstead water mill built in 1789 and burnt down in 1963.

37. Horstead Common between the church and the river was used as a 'drying ground' by the local women to dry cloths. There was another 'drying ground' just over the bridge in Coltishall also on common ground.

38. Present limit of hire boat navigation although the Broads Society installed a boat slide for open boats. The Site of first lock of the Aylesham Navigation which was built between 1773-79 although there had been commercial traffic up the upper Bure long before this. The navigation was created by fitting locks and digging new channels round watermills. The Aylesham Navigation was commercialy successful until the 1880s when the railways reached eastern Norfolk. In the Flood of 1912, caused by very heavy rain falling in a few hours, the Navigation was very badly damaged and had to be closed.

RIVER THURNE

39. Hunter's Yard. In 1932 Percy Hunter and his sons Cyril and Stan opened a boat yard here. They built a fleet of eighteen varnished sailing hire craft. In 1968 the Hunter family sold the yard and hire fleet to the Norfolk County Council. The Hunter boats were not modernised, but there was a public outcry when the NCC decided to sell the yard and boats. In 1996 the Norfolk Heritage Fleet Trust took over Hunters yard and its 15 engineless, gaff cruising yacht.

40. Colin Buttifant, Yacht and Boatbuilder moved here from Ludham in 1994.

41. Womack Water. Formerly open water cut off from the river, but a dyke had been cut up to Ludham for wherries. The open Womack Water was overgrown by 1887. Last regatta about 1910 and then the event was moved to Thurne Mouth. The channel behind the island became silted up but was reopened in 1978.

42. Robert Harrison's boat yard which had a slip for wherries closed in 1892. This was half way between the island and the Maltings Staithe.

43. In 1890 there was a dyke right up to the Staithe Road where wherries discharged straight into carts which stood on the road. A local land owner closed this staithe and the dyke silted up. Reed island at the head of Womack Water was dredged out about 1965.

44. Repps Staithe. In the early nineteenth century most of the keels on the northern waters were owned in Repps.

45. Broads Haven was started by Herbert Woods in 1936 when he moved his yard from the other side of the bridge.

46. Potter Heigham Staithe was used by wherries. Urbanised by the Broads Authority.

47. In 1897 F.E.Chambers bought land around Potter Heigham Bridge. In 1901 he opened a Norfolk Broads Yacht Co boatyard here with the work force from Mollet's yard at Brundall which he had closed. Walter Woods who was manager of the NBY yard bought the yard in 1920. Walter died in 1928 and his sons Walter and Herbert took over.

48. In 1895 George Applegate started the first boatyard at Potter Heigham, above the bridge. The Applegate sheds were pulled down by the Broads Authority around 1994. The Bridge Hotel opposite burned down in 1993. Applegates Staithe is on a dyke on the eastern shore below the bridge.

49. The Great Yarmouth and Stalham Light Railway bridge over the Thurne at Potter Heigham was opened in 1883 and closed in 1959. Later the site was used for the Potter Heigham bypass road.

50. Two eel setts in Heigham Sound. In 1995 the Broads Authority only allowed one eel man to operate here.

51. Martham Ferry ownership goes with the farm.

52. Meadow Dike appears to be a made man dyke linking Horsey to Heigham Sound. Before World War I the meadows on either side were neat. They were cut every summer for sedge 'marsh litter' which went on the railway to London where it was used in the stables. Until the mid-1950s there was a tow path so that wherries and yachts could be hauled along, but once engines became general this path grew over.

53. The Horsey Estate was bought from the Buxton family in 1948 by the National Trust. Horsey Mere was dredged in the late 1960s.

54. The Staithe Stores was started on Horsey Staithe in the 1920s and was run by the village until being taken over by the National Trust in 1991. Horsey pump mill was built in 1912 and worked until it was struck by lightning in 1943.

55. Brograve Level. Village of Waxham Parve washed away in a great storm of 1791. The Lord of the Manor Sir Barney Brograve (1726-1797) had these marshes drained and walled off.

56. Waxham New Cut was dug as a drainage channel by Brograve in about 1785. Only small wherries could get up to Lound Staithe at Lound Bridge, Sea Palling and then they often towed a reed lighter so that if they got struck, part of the cargo could be off loaded. There was also a brick works here and wherries turned round at the first bend. Last wherry working up here was the 20 ton *Zulu* until about 1900.

57. Brograve Bridge. The New Cut was dammed off just above the bridge, but a wherry continued to bring 21 tons of coal up to the bridge for Lambridge steam pump mill. Ernie Johnson started a boat yard here with a hire fleet at the Bridge.

58. Hickling Priory founded in 1185. In the thirteenth century a causeway was built to link it to the road. In 1287 the sea flooded this area and the Priory seems to have fallen on hard times.

59. Hickling Wall. This appears to be a medieval sea wall built as a second line of defence against flooding from the sea. The area around here was drained about 1750 to create better grazing marshes.

60. Whiteslea Lodge. Because Hickling was regarded by the Victorians as being a very good winter duck shoot a lodge was built here, but this burnt down about 1867. Around 1905 Lord Lucas built a new Whiteslea Lodge for duck shooting. In 1945 the Norfolk Naturalists bought Hickling and subsequently made Whiteslea their headquarters.

61. Roland Green's Mill. The well known bird painter Roland Green had a studio in the old mill.

62. Hickling Sailing Clubhouse was built in 1960 with a thatched roof in the style of the boat houses on the Common.

63. Whispering Reed boat hire yard at Hickling took over Waldo Beales yard. Waldo had started his small day boat and fishing boat hire business here in about 1930. He was a true Broadsman involved in everything from duck shooting to founding the Hickling Sailing Club and is reputed to have never sworn.

64. Catfield Wood End staithe was opened in about 1968 with help from Hoseason's

65. Rose Farm Staithe used by wherries until around 1870 when a rhond (Norfolk name for a river wall) was built cutting Rose Farm Staithe off from Hickling Broad

RIVER ANT

66. Hundred Dike is believed to be the old course of the Ant in the Anglo-Saxon period.

67. Ludham Bridge replaced the former arched bridge in about 1928.

68. Reedham Marsh. The original course of the Ant ran in a bend to the west of How Hill. Some time before 1797 the course of the river was straightened to run along its present course.

69. Fen Turf windmill was built in about 1880 to lower the water level on Reedham Marshes. Reedham Water had been part of the old course of the Ant when it bent round along the west side of the valley. Some time before 1797 the river took its present course. This change of course resulted in Reedham Water growing up with reeds, but in about 1990 this was cleaned out for conservation.

70. How Hill Staithe. The 1802 Ludham Enclosure Act allowed the land around the staithe to go into private ownership. A windmill was built in 1825 on the high ground to grind the corn grown on the land which had been developed for farming.

71. How Hill. In 1904 the Norwich architect Edward Boardman pulled down the windmill on top of the hill and built How Hill as a family home in his 872 acre estate. Boardman completely altered the area by planting 70000 trees which turned the valley from open grazing to a wooded landscape. The Boardmans sold How Hill to the Norfolk County Council in 1966, but the expense of keeping it up resulted in them selling the house to the Norwich Union in 1984 who leased it to the How Hill Trust.

72. Boardman's Mill. Trestle smock pump mill Built about 1910 to drain the Clayrack Marshes so that they could be cut of sedge in the summer and reed in the winter while the better land was grazed by cattle. After the bad Floods of 1912 most of the Broads drainage systems which had been built up in the previous century were destroyed. Because of changes in farming much of the Ant valley was left to grow wild.

73. Crome's Broad. This appears to have been dug for turbary (local name for peat) around 1383. All the medieval peat digging areas gradually filled with water.

74. Catfield Fen became a reserve to save East Anglia's swallow tailed butterfly in 1992.

75. Irstead Shoal Staithe owned by Barton Turf Charity.

76. Thrower's boat yard was at Carrow Green staithe until 1939.

77. During World War II the wherry *Cornucopia* and other craft rotted away moored on Barton Broad to prevent a German invasion form landing in sea planes. In 1995 the Broads Authority started a major dredging programme to return Barton Broad to the depth of six foot so that it could be used for sailing again. The spoil was pumped out on to adjoining farm land and used to make up Pleasure Hill Island. Turkey Broad, the bottom end of Barton, was used to store the fish while dredging took place.

78. Wherry Arches at the head of dyke beside Gay's Dyke leading off the Lime Kiln Dyke. The Wherry Arches were part of Grove Farm, a late eighteenth century set of red brick buildings. Wherries came underneath this granary until about 1928. It then became derelict and over grown with ivy and in about 1971 was converted to holiday homes.

79. The Cox family built wherries at Barton until 1894. Hulk of the pleasure wherry *Victory*.

80. Sutton Broad was open water in 1840, but the reeds and trees grew right across it. The dyke up to the farm was kept open and in 1928 Basil Hitching opened the Staithe Farm Hotel.

81. From 1957-59 a yacht harbour was dug on the Stalham horse grazing marshes.

82. Cooke's Staithe has a Granary built in 1808 over the head of the dyke. This was built so that small wherries could go underneath it. The granary was used for grass seeds, no wherrys here after 1920. In 1977 the Granary was converted to a house for the Dent family. In 1995 Michael Burton was still using the sheds opposite for his coal merchants business. He remembered the last wherry to deliver coal here was the *Cornucopia* in 1939. The Public Staithe opposite Burton's was also used for unloading coal.

83. The dyke up to Dilham brick works under the bridge was dug out in 1810 . When the Ant Navigation was opened Israel Lewis successfully sued the navigation company for the loss of trade which had formerly gone over his staithe to North Walsham. Dilham Staithe became silted up after the wherry traffic finished and the section up to the Brick Kiln Bridge was bought by the East Anglian Waterways Association and dredged in 1965. A new staithe was created at the top. Before this hire craft had been going up to Honing Bridge to turn round but this river was left to silt up.

84. The eight and half mile Ant Navigation or North Walsham & Dilham Canal was dug between 1812-26. Small 18-20 ton slipping keel wherries traded right up to Antingham Ponds, but the canal was never a commercial success. P.H.Emerson just managed to get his pleasure wherry *Maid of the Mist* up to Antingham Ponds in 1890. The navigation was badly damaged by the 1912 Flood and the upper section was abandoned in 1927. Last cargo up to Bacton Wood Staithe in 1936.

River Bure

River Ant

River Thurne

Thurne Mouth

Hundred Stream

River Bure

Chapter Four
FROM YARMOUTH TOWN TO KING'S LYNN

TOWN HALL AND RIVER, GT. YARMOUTH.

125. The Gorleston lifeboat *John and Mary Meiklam of Gladswood*, a motor lifeboat built in 1922, going out with the huge fleet of Scottish steam drifters in about 1938. At this time there were 725 drifters fishing out of Yarmouth giving employment to about 6000 people. Even after World II it was a common sight to see hundreds of drifters at the Yarmouth quays. By 1953 the fleet was down to 331 drifters and this number dropped rapidly as over fishing emptied the North Sea. This happened because mid-water trawling was introduced which took all the herring shoals.

Opposite Top. 123. Barges and wherries at Great Yarmouth in 1928. The first Haven Bridge was built in 1417 replacing a horse ferry. The wherry on the right has a steel hull.

Yarmouth developed as a fishing centre in the medieval period and since every property owner wished to have part of the all important waterfront on the Yare, the land was owned in narrow strips. When the population grew these strips of property were built over, leaving only very narrow alleys, known as Rows, between them. The old town Yarmouth was unique with its 145 Rows cutting through the densely packed houses.

Charles Dickens visited Yarmouth in 1848-49 and was clearly impressed by this incredible town. Later Victorian painters also came to the area because Yarmouth had the feeling of a medieval town. Because of the railway link to the cities Yarmouth became a major holiday resort and many visitors first explored the Broads from here. Much of the old town was destroyed after 1933 when the council started to pull down the Rows to make wider roads and better housing.

Opposite Bottom. 124. The paddle tug *Express* towing the sailing trawlers out of Yarmouth Haven's Mouth in 1889. The man in the pulling boat on the right would have been a member of one of the Gorleston Beach Companies who helped sailing ships in and out of the port.

Yarmouth developed as a trawling station after the Barking and Brixham smacks landed their catches here. About 1854 Samuel Hewett moved his fleet of smacks from Barking to Gorleston. In 1890 the large trawler fleets, the Columbia and Hewett's Short Blue, joined forces to supply the London market with cheap fish. The trawling smacks were mostly company owned in Yarmouth but early in the 1900s most of these companies collapsed which ended the towns era as a major trawling centre.

126. Two Scottish herring drifters putting to sea from Yarmouth in about 1935. Every autumn the drifters from the east coast of Scotland came south to join in the herring fishery. In 1930 when the 104ft Yarmouth drifter *Lydia Eva* was built at King's Lynn for Harry Eastick most people thought the herring shoals were inexhaustible. *Lydia Eva* survived after the end of the East Anglian herring fishery because she was sold to the Admiralty. Long afterwards it was realized that she was the only surviving steam drifter.

127. Landing the herrings at the Fishwharf, Yarmouth in about 1935. In the back ground is the Retort Tower of the Gorleston & Southtown Gas Company. This Tower was demolished in 1967.

128. The steam herring drifter *Wydale YH 105* putting to sea from Yarmouth in 1959. She was last drifter working from Yarmouth and finished the following year.

129. In the days when people walked to work there were eleven ferries over the Yare and Wensum, but in 1996 only the Lower Ferry at Gorleston and Cantley ferry remained. The Lower Ferry to Yarmouth was started about 1100 and was a rowing ferry until motor boats were introduced in 1956. While workers went across to the Bird's Eye factory around 1700 people used it every week. However numbers of passengers started to drop and in 1974, for the first time since the medieval ferry started, there was no ferry at the weekends. It had to rely on local government support to keep the service open.

130. Four sailing shrimpers entering Yarmouth. The first Yarmouth shrimpers were open rowing boats working off the beach in front of the town. About 1870 sailing shrimpers where built to work out of the harbour. These were the only British workboats to have a single jib, an idea that originated from the Broads yachts. The shrimpers worked in the summer, sailing to sea every morning and returning midday so that the brown shrimps could be cooked ashore and sold for afternoon tea. Fishermen often had a boiler in their back yard and sold the shrimps from their homes.

131. The 21ft Yarmouth shrimper *Coronation* towing a yacht on Breydon Water about 1926. Built in 1902 at the time of King Edward's coronation this shrimper was acquired by the Maritime Museum at Yarmouth in about 1976 and became part of their important collection of Norfolk boats.

132. Fred Symonds getting his shrimp trawl aboard his 22ft *Crangon* off Yarmouth beach in 1989. Fred Symonds started shrimp trawling with his father in 1926. Just before World War II they sold their larger shrimper and bought the *Horace & Hannah* which Fred worked until he had the *Crangon* built in 1957.

About 1938 Yarmouth church was badly damaged by fire and some English oak, then about seven hundred years old, was salvaged from the roof. Nearly twenty years later it was taken to Gus Lee and Boswell's yard at Runham Vauxhall and used to build the *Crangon* and a year later the *Boy Frank*. In 1996 only Chris Moore was doing a little shrimping with *Boy Frank* while the *Crangon* was bought out of fishing by the author's son Jonathan.

133. The British barque *Marques* leaving Yarmouth and heading out through the Hewett Channel for the start of the 1978 Tall Ships Race to southern Norway. The *Marques* was very sadly lost with all eleven people aboard after leaving the West Indies.

134. The MTB *102* off Yarmouth on the way to watch the start of the 1978 Tall Ships Race. This motor torpedo boat was built at Vospers in 1938 and had a single torpedo tube. After World War II she became the headquarters of the Ist Blofield and Brundall Sea Scouts and was stationed on the Broads. She was made seaworthy again for the film 'When Eagles have Landed'.

135. The Hemsby inshore inflatable lifeboat at the fund raising Herring Festival in 1995. In 1841 a group of Winterton fishermen moved south and established a beach company at Hemsby which they called Newport. A beach company was a fisherman's cooperative which operated beach yawls used for salvaging ships in distress. The beach companies were replaced by the RNLI lifeboats, but there was never a lifeboat based at Hemsby.

From about 1922 holiday chalets were built near the wonderful sandy beaches and there were some sad cases of holiday makers getting drowned. This resulted in local people keeping a rescue boat on the beach. In 1975 an inshore life boat was bought and manned by local volunteers. The Hemsby Inshore Lifeboat house was built in 1988 250 metres inshore of the high tide mark, but by 1995 the encroaching sea had eaten its way inland so that a high tide had washed away the ramp of the boat house.

Caister had an RNLI lifeboat operating until 1969, when it was believed that the new fast Gorleston lifeboat could cover the whole coast. However local people formed the Caister Volunteer Rescue Service which bought its own deep water lifeboat in 1971.

136. Coal being discharged from the billyboy *Angerona* in the River Glaven at Cley-next-the-Sea in about 1870. This was at the new port of Cley created after the original estuary had silted up. In the medieval period the Glaven was tidal nearly up to Letheringsett and ships reached the quays at Wiveton and at Newton Green, Cley. When the quays at Newton Green silted up a river wall was put across to closed off the upper Glaven in 1823. Following this the area around the windmill was developed as a small port with slipway, quay and a granary. Silting continued and trade slowly died away and finished in 1914.

137. The windmill at Cley in about 1950 when this part of the Glaven was still tidal water. Cley seems such a tranquil place, disturbed only by the east wind and summer tourists, that it is easy to overlook the dramatic changes the sea has made to this coast. The medieval port of Cley, which sent ships to the Icelandic fishery, sat on the wide Glaven estuary. The entrance to the Glaven was at Cley Eye with channels leading off either side to Salthouse and Blakeney. Over the centuries the sea has relentlessly torn away the soft coast and at the same time blocked up the Cley Eye. Only very occasionally does the sea do something really dramatic and take a whole village in a storm. Norfolk has slipped into the sea a few feet at a time. As it happens slowly many think it is unavoidable, however in the twentieth century sea defences have proved that it is possible to stop erosion. If such sea defences had existed from Roman times Norfolk would have been a very much larger county. The sea has taken the land people have lived on.

138. Coastal trading ships at Blakeney about 1880. In the middle of this group of ships discharging at the quay are the two lighters which were used for off loading cargoes. With the lighter draft, ships were then able to reach the quay. On the right are some of the Blakeney canoes, flat bottom punts, used in the shell fishery. Around this time thirty men had shellfish layings in Blakeney Harbour and the Cley Channel. This died out and the last of the canoes were laying around Blakeney in the early 1980s.

The Carnser, Blakeney.

84408

139. The Carnser at Blakeney in about 1936. The holiday trade had already taking over the quay and boat trips down to Blakeney Head were already well established, while mussel gathering was just ending.

140. Bare footed women gathering the 'Stewkey Blues' cockles on the cold open coastal flats in 1904. In 1875 about hundred women were cultivating cockles in lays at Stiffkey, once pronouced Stewkey. In 1909 there were still about thirty women walking out from the village across the marshes as the tide went down and then digging out cockles with a bent knife. The women on the left has one of these knives in her hand.

Brancaster Staithe   84362

141. Brancaster Staithe in about 1951. Until 1900 there were about twenty smacks oyster dredging from Brancaster. The last boat to dredge from here was the double ended *Pelican* until 1935 and her hull still lay in the mud to the left of this view fifty years later.

Brancaster Harbour is clean because there are no towns in the area. It is good for shelfish because of the calcium bearing freshwater that flows into it. While most of the other fisheries have considerably decreased, in 1984 there were still nine people mussel fishing here. The cockles and mussels are collected from the Wash off Hunstanton and brought into Brancaster Harbour in the summer. Here they are put on 'lays' for a year and then sold during the winter.

144. The little Lynn smack *Mary True* in Heacham Harbour about 1920. The houseboats in Heacham Harbour became the 'lost fleet' after the harbour was closed off in 1933. Before this Capt Drew towed round the barge *Ernest George*, smack *Doris* and Scottish lugger *Violet* to become houseboats. The shingle had to be dug away from the mouth to get them in. In the 1953 Floods some of the houseboats floated away out of the channel.

The last commercial vessel visited Burnham Overy Staithe in 1916 and it was not until 1996 that the next one, the barge *Cabby*, came in for a wedding reception.

Opposite Top. 142. Brancaster shell fisherman Leonard Loose at Brancaster Staithe in 1984 with one of the flat bottomed mussel boats built by Worfolks.

In the back ground is the Yarmouth yoll *Amity* which was built to run pleasure trips off the beach. She was damaged by shell fire from the German Navy during 1916. The damaged *Amity* was bought by William Loose who had her repaired by the Worfolks and then he used her for mussel gathering at Brancaster. After William Loose died in 1960 his son Leonard and grandson John sold *Amity* and the Worfolks built the 35ft *Melita* for them. The *Amity* was the last of the large East Anglian sailing beach boats and later became a yacht.

Opposite Bottom. 143. The Kings Lynn smack *Rob Pete* ready for relaunching at Wells-Next-The-Sea after being rebuilt by William Cracknell in 1994. The *Rob Pete* was built in 1924 to go shrimping in the summer and shell fishing in the winter. One of her builders Bill Worfolk was then nearly a hundred years old and on this particular day could not brave the cold to see her relaunched. He must have been the last of the English smack builders.

Standing near the smack is Lynn fisherman Peter Garrett and his family, which include his sons Rob and Pete after whom he renamed the smack during the time he owned her.

Fishing Fleet, King's Lynn

145. About thirty smacks lying in Fisher Fleet, Kings Lynn in about 1935. The original Fisher Fleet was at the north side of the medieval town. When the Alexandra Dock was constructed in 1869 the present Fisher Fleet was dug just outside the dock area. Few fish enter the narrow channels of the Wash, the local fleet work for shellfish and shrimp.

146. The sailing barge *Will Everard* loading 240 tons of Norfolk wheat in the Purfleet, King's Lynn for the Co-op Mills at Hull in 1955.

That autumn Everards had a contract to move wheat to Hull. The author sailed on the *Will Everard* and remembers that about once a week a local man used to come down in thigh boots at low tide and shovel the silt into the gut way to be washed away. It seems that when ships no longer came to Purfleet to load, this practice stopped and the berths silted up. In 1986 the Baltic ketch *Dania* was brought into Purfleet for the making of the film 'Revolution' and was abandoned there. In 1996 the Council decided to break up the wrecks in the Purfleet.

147. Bill Worfolk and Frank Castleton beside the 37ft ketch *Lady of Lynn,* the last craft the Worfolk Brothers built, in 1975.

Thomas Worfolk had started building wooden ships at Kings Lynn after he moved from Yorkshire in 1899. His first craft the Norfolk yoll *Baden Powell* was launched the following year. After this he built a series of powerful sailing smacks to fish out of Lynn. The *Nellie & Leslie* in 1911, the *Freda & Norah* in 1912 and the 58ft *Britannia* in 1913. Their largest smack and the first vessel to be built at Lynn with an engine, was the *Grace & Edna* in 1916. These Wash smacks had very fine bows to make them manoeuvrable in the narrow channels. The smacks also had attractive rounded counter sterns. The yard was later run by Thomas' sons Gerald and Bill.

Because these craft worked in the sheltered waters of the Wash many of the wooden sailing smacks had very long working careers. In 1994 Ron Fisher, whose family had the *Baden Powell* built, was still using her for 'sand topping' for cockles, and the *Queen Alexandra*, a shrimper the Worfolks built to win the Lynn smack races, was still working.

148. Peter Chase, one of Len Bone's partners, hand raking cockles in the Wash in 1981.

In the Victorian period, when there were 120 boats at Lynn, cockles were gathered in the summer by hand raking on the sands at low water. When power boats came in a method known as ploughing was used. Boats went out on a falling tide and anchored on the sands and then tried to 'plough' round in a circle which stirred up the cockles which were then hand raked.

In 1986 the Eastern Sea Fisheries, who attempt to control fishing in the Wash, allowed suction dredgers to gather cockles. The boats with suction dredgers work at high water and are very efficient, but require high capital investment. In 1995, 68 boats were registered at Lynn. About half these boats were shrimping in the summer and the others cockling, but only two of them were using the old ploughing method. The winter fishery is mussels which are gathered with large dredges towed along the sea bed. Around 1990 there was a great bonanza in the Wash mussel fishery followed by a scarcity. In fishing, like everything else, the conditions are constantly changing.

150. Len Bone's boat being loaded with cockles in the Wash in 1981.

151. Wildfowlers taking birds from their nets in the Wash in 1905. The taking of wildfowl for sale, by netting, was stopped in 1954 by a law.

152. The South Quay at King's Lynn with the Humber billyboy *Evening Star* and two other vessels being loaded by hand with goods carried along planks about 1904.

153. Lynn smack *Victor* laid up in a creek in West Lynn about 1900.

38th Gramophone Concert

Saturday 11th July 1931

Programme

1. Suite No. 2 in B minor *Bach*
   1. 2. Overture
   3. Rondeau; Sarabande; Bourée
   4. Polonaise and Double; Minuet; Badinerie

Chicago Symphony Orchestra under Frederick Stock

2. Symphony No. 6 in G major *"Surprise"* *Haydn*
   1. 2. Adagio cantabile — Allegro vivace
   3. 4. Andante
   5. Allegro molto
   6. Allegro di molto

Boston Symphony Orchestra under Serge Koussevitsky

INTERVAL

3. Symphony No. 35 in D major *"Haffner"* *Mozart*
   1. 2a. Allegro con spirito
   2b. 3. Andante
   4. Menuetto
   5. Finale — Presto

*Philharmonic Symphony Orchestra of New York
under Arturo Toscanini*

4. Symphony No. 7 in A major. Op. 92. *Beethoven*
   1. 2. 3. Poco sostenuto; Vivace
   4. 5. 6. Allegretto
   7. 8. Presto
   9. 10. Allegro con brio

Philadelphia Symphony Orchestra under Leopold Stokowski